# THE SPECTACULAR
# ORDINARY LIFE

# THE SPECTACULAR ORDINARY LIFE

## Experiencing Full, Vivid and Rich Life

**Viv Thomas**

**Authentic**

MILTON KEYNES • COLORADO SPRINGS • HYDERABAD

This edition published 2008 by Authentic Media
9 Holdom Avenue, Bletchley, Milton Keynes, MK1 1QR, UK
1820 Jet Stream Drive, Colorado Springs, CO 80921, USA
OM Authentic Media, Medchal Road, Jeedimetla Village,
Secunderabad 500 055, A.P., India
www.authenticmedia.co.uk

Authentic Media is a division of IBS-STL U.K., limited by guarantee, with its
Registered Office at Kingstown Broadway, Carlisle, Cumbria CA3 0HA.
Registered in England & Wales No. 1216232. Registered charity 270162

**British Library Cataloguing in Publication Data**
A catalogue record for this book is available from the British Library

ISBN-13: 978-1-85078-791-4

Design by James Kessell for Scratch the Sky Ltd (www.scratchthesky.com)
Print Management by Adare
Printed in Great Britain by J.H. Haynes & Co., Sparkford

This book is dedicated to Sheila Thomas, who has made my ordinary spectacular for over thirty years

For whoever wants to save his life will lose it, but whoever loses his life for me will find it.
Jesus Christ
Matthew 16:25

I have come that they may have life, and have it to the full.
Jesus Christ
John 10:10

In him was life, and that life was the light of men.
John 1:4

# Contents

# Acknowledgements

Huge thanks goes to: Patrick Harrison; Jan Truesdale; Rowena Chiu; Emily Radcliffe; Rupert Edwards; Mark Powley; Lucy Hawes; Simon Downham; Ian Stackhouse; Adam Baron; Rachel and Adam Winn; Richard and Sally Worley; Mel and Adrian Self; Richard and Lydia Evans; Hugh and Leslie Reynolds; Chris and Joanna Frizelle; David and Jennifer Allison; George Verwer; Don Simpson; Eugene Peterson; Mike Sherwood, all the supporters of Formation, the staff team, and members of St. Paul's Hammersmith. Ruth Cameron, Kate White and Sheila Thomas have been critical, creative and brilliant throughout this project.

# Foreword

You have in your hands an unusual book, and I hope you will take the time to read it as I have. I have known Viv and his wife, Sheila, for over thirty years and I have seen the dynamic message of this book lived out in their lives.

The central focus of this book is the Lord Jesus himself, and Viv brings out the life message of Jesus in a powerful and beautiful way – some very fresh thoughts and ideas.

If you want an overall glimpse of what you are getting into, please take a glance at Chapter Thirteen. Here is a summary of what the spectacular ordinary life is all about. If you will take this book seriously, it could revolutionize your life and you will discover a new way to walk in God's grace and power.

Too many books today are trying to give neat, tidy answers to hyper-complex challenges and situations. Here is a book for messy situations and for people like me, who don't have their act together and yet are experiencing this life in Christ every day (as I have for fifty-two years).

Please read it prayerfully and in a spirit of openness and faith. Maybe you're not a Christian, or you are loaded with doubts. Then this is also the book for you.

*George Verwer*

# Introduction

It is seven o'clock in the morning and I am in dreamland. I am sitting on a hill just above Malibu, California, and looking out over the Pacific Ocean. This is West Coast USA, and the dream of the good life that spread out from Europe and through North America becomes a reality here.

This is a beautiful place inhabited by impossibly perfect beings. Film and rock stars glide around in their expensive cars, from fashionable bar to restaurant to mall. Appearance is everything here; how you look, what you wear, where you're seen. You need to be conscious of your own life on a moment-by-moment basis to make sure you send the right messages of wealth, beauty, success and happiness. To be ordinary is almost unacceptable.

Life in Malibu seems to encapsulate everything we dream of achieving; an image that proclaims to the world that these people have 'made it'. It is as though all the values deeply held by so many of us become vividly real in this wonderful location.

But, for all its glittering promise, the longed-for life cannot truly deliver. All is not well in paradise. Even this Utopia is not free from poverty and sickness. Shattered families, drug rehab centres, huge debt problems and superficial relationships and conversations speak of the reality at the heart of the dream. But before we talk about life and what could possibly have gone wrong with us, I want to talk about the opposite of life; death.

When I was sixteen, my grandmother died. I know that for many people the death of a grandparent is a devastating experience. This was not the case for me. I hardly knew my mother's mother, and what I did know was minimal. She was a widow from Liverpool and my mother didn't get on with her.

For example, my mother and I once visited grandmother in a residential home in Liverpool. Mum took her two gifts. The first was a bottle of Warninks Advocaat. Mum knew that her mother did not like it and so the gift would be returned, ensuring that she could drink it peacefully at home. However, the second gift was a real stunner; a gift so memorable and so shocking that I doubt if anyone in the home would be able to forget the day my mother came to visit. The gift was a dead sheep's head.

Soon after we arrived, my grinning mother presented the sheep's head to grandmother and began to howl with laughter. Mum so enjoyed the joke that, before grandmother could even take in what she had been given, my mother took hold of the head and, using the greaseproof paper as a tray, paraded the head around the home. She looked like some ancient Roman conqueror, back from battle with the spoils of war.

She was so enthused by the whole thing that she pushed this head close to the faces of Liverpool's aged and told them to have a look. She didn't notice that some of them were asleep, and on waking to her noise, opened their eyes to the empty eye sockets of a dead sheep.

So, there was grandmother being visited by her own daughter and receiving two gifts; one she did not want, and the other a joke. I must have some gift of discretion, or a strong sense of survival, because I did not tell Sheila this story until after we were married!

When my grandmother died, only my mother and I attended her funeral, along with a few other distant family members whom we rarely saw. I have never been to a funeral like it, and I hope for all concerned that I never go to one like it again.

Just before Mum left home, aged fourteen, to go into domestic service, she went to the movies with her younger sister and gave her a note to pass to their mother explaining that she would not be coming home. She left home in her own unique way, and she attended her mother's funeral in similar style.

My mother's side of the family were Roman Catholic, so the funeral was to be Catholic. Someone had decided that there would be a short service in a chapel at the graveyard and then, after a short procession, grandmother would be buried.

When my mother and I turned up at the chapel there were no family members, hearse or priest. I presumed that we would just wait a few minutes until everyone else arrived. This was not Mum's intention. She decided that she needed a good strong drink, and promptly announced that she wasn't going to wait around and was off to the pub. She turned, clutched her coat to her body and was gone.

The inevitable happened. Within ten minutes the car, coffin, family and priest all arrived but there was no Mum. We stood and waited. She came up the path with a face set like a bulldog and her first words to her grieving sister were 'All the bloody pubs are closed.' I was beginning to see why the rest of the family kept away from us. I knew we were in for a particularly challenging and dramatic time, but there was nothing new in that.

My mother missed her drink, and, in her own way, she must have been upset. But it was difficult for me to understand what was going on. I was into deep family history, watching the feelings surface but knowing few of the facts that triggered those feelings. However, one great overarching problem was starting to surface; my mother's love of theatre. She always insisted that she was the centre of attention, wherever and whenever it was available. If she did not get centre stage, she had her ways of just grabbing the limelight for herself. She had no intention of letting her dead mother be the star at her own funeral; there was only going to be one queen at the ball, one actress on the stage, and that was herself. It was emerging that Mum was going to win.

We followed the coffin into the cold, damp church and, feeling that the next twenty minutes could be seriously bizarre, I decided to take control. As Mum was about to walk in after the coffin, I grabbed her by the elbow and held on. She struggled, but I held her back to the end of the line. By the age of sixteen I was already much taller and considerably stronger than my mother. It seemed important to me that she was not on the front row, but at the back. I anticipated, quite wrongly as it turned out, that she would not be the centre of attention if I kept her at the back.

The priest started to chant and swing incense and my mother started to laugh. This was not belly-laughter, but rather tongue-and-lip laughter. She was famous for this laugh, and it came out of her mouth like a stuttering puncture on a bike tyre. It was a siss . . . siss . . . siss sound which echoed around the cavern of the chapel. If you put your head in a big bell and made the sound, you would get the same effect. In between fits of this she would sigh. The sighs were so loud that you could not hear what the priest was saying. It was a get-on-with-it sigh, an 'I'm bored' sigh, and we all got the message.

Grandmother, nil: mother, one.

When we left the church, I held onto Mum's elbow again. She complained, but I didn't let go. I wanted to create distance between ourselves and the funeral party; I thought about fifty yards would do it. She struggled to get away, but I made sure we didn't walk up the wet shingle path between the graves until I was ready. However, my problem was that the whole event was becoming so uncontrolled and bizarre that I was beginning to find the whole thing funny. I am, after all, my mother's son.

We walked slowly, about thirty to forty yards behind everyone else, and then the right heel on Mum's stiletto shoe suddenly snapped. She fell to the ground like an imploding chimney; she seemed to collapse straight down, driving into the dirt. Her knees hit the wet shingle and she rolled over to the side of the path. We both began to laugh. Lip laughter was gone – this was now laughter so deep that it seemed to force its way from the pit of the stomach before it erupted in an explosion of sound.

I tried to lift her up but her body was limp with laughter. She had torn her stockings and her right knee was a mixture of water, blood and mud encrusted with little stones. I put my arm around her waist and held her as we walked towards the funeral party; both of us had faces stained with tears of laughter rather than grief. To make matters worse, Mum now walked with a pronounced and comical limp that radically slowed our progress. By the time we finally arrived at the graveside, all eyes were on us.

Grandmother, nil: mother, two.

It was at this point that the priest realized that there were no ropes to lower the coffin into the grave, and called for an assistant to go and get them from the last funeral. The assistant ran off, with his Wellington boots flicking up the mud behind him, and, obviously embarrassed, the priest tried to make polite conversation to fill these moments with meaning. He should have said nothing. Glancing at the few people around the grave he asked 'Are these the only relatives this poor lady had?' Before anyone else could answer, my mother took control of the conversation. 'She was no poor old lady, she was a wicked old woman,' she declared. We all stood in an uncomfortable silence, waiting for the ropes, and the priest only opened his mouth again to utter the formal sentences in his black book and a few basic instructions.

Grandmother, nil: mother, three.

At the end of the funeral the priest gave everyone around the grave a handful of dirt. Before we left we were to walk to the grave and throw the dirt onto the successfully lowered coffin. I knew this meant another opportunity for drama and trouble. The priest had just given my mother a prop to act out a final flourish. It was like giving Billy the Kid fresh bullets. Of course, he had no idea that he was dealing with the visionary and implementer of the sheep's head drama.

I held onto Mum hoping that we could do our dirt-throwing last while the others wandered away. But they did not wander; they just waited. This gave my mother her final opportunity, and she took it with such dramatic ease that in retrospect I cannot help but admire her. With every eye on us we lurched to the graveside and she threw her dirt. Everyone else had let go of their handful in a humble downward fashion, letting it drop from the hand into the grave and, after a few moments, stepping back. This was not Mum's intention or style. She took the dirt and, with a look of exultation, propelled it skywards. It was a Muhammad Ali motion, a boxer's uppercut, with more of the earth missing the hole than hitting it. It was like the final salute; the final act of defiance; the final act of victory, and everyone saw it happen.

Grandmother, nil: mother, four.

All I knew at the time was that on the day of my grandmother's funeral, life and death were being played out. I was in the middle of deep family mysteries and Mum never told me what they were. Why the battle? Why the competition? What could have caused such a response to the death of your mother? Somewhere along the line there was a deficit of life.

This is the theatre of Jesus Christ, for, right at the centre of our beings and relationships, we need life. It is only in God that we become fully alive and are able to step out of all the various kinds of death. It is in these sorts of family dirt-hard relationships that the Spirit brings life: spectacular ordinary life.

Yet our culture leads us to believe that life is easy. It is a cool, clear, calm experience in which you focus on your dreams and work out how you are going to fulfil them.

Life is success. It is the theatre for self-articulation where all your potential is gathered and focused, enabling you to enjoy the fruit of your many gifts and abilities.

Life is pleasure. It is the setting for as many warm feelings and sweet sensations as possible, all packed into the short time available.

Life is beauty. To live your life well, you need to be young and beautiful; but if you aren't either, then you can fake it.

This is the world portrayed to us through television, much of the media and advertising in general, and celebrated in countless bars, coffee shops, dinner parties and work conversations throughout the urban world. These industries have considerable self-interest in making us believe that they can provide us with everything to ensure we live easy, successful, pleasurable and beautiful lives. To attain this quartet of interlocking ideas costs money, most of which goes into their pockets.

The phenomenon that most clearly demonstrates these values is the cult of celebrity. We spend our time focusing on the lives of stars who we believe live spectacular and exciting lives. They come from the world of film, sport, fashion, and music; initially captivating, and eventually holding a vice-like grip on our hearts. Like children focused on the jangling noise of the ice-cream van, we respond every time we hear the mood-creating music of celebrity, and head off running towards the sound.

Then along comes Jesus and, as always, messes up our fantasy of coordinated and manicured lives so that he can put them back together in a sane way. He raises awkward questions at the wrong time, twists things around so we don't recognize them any more, and leads us into paradoxes that we prefer not to have.

It is no wonder that we can become so angry with him, for who is he to do this to us? Who is he to tell us that the first shall be last and the last first, that meek people inherit the earth, that the way to make something of your life is to lose it? What sort of strange magic is this? How can the contemporary world with its focus on ease, success, pleasure and beauty come together with the different world Jesus has pointed us towards?

That is the arena in which this book will operate, by exploring some central truths that go right to the foundations of how we live our lives. We will be looking at some huge realities, without which our lives cannot work as they are intended to. These are all articulated in one way or another through Christian Scripture.

Living a spectacular ordinary life is the theme of this book and we will interact with that idea throughout. To be a Christian is to be fully alive in every dimension of life. There is nothing – absolutely nothing – that is outside of this sort of life. Hate, love, deceit, gentleness, ambition, desire, humour, sex, illness, hunger, food, the body, aging, death, material possessions, and much more besides are all part of being alive.

Shakespeare does life well. In the summer of 2005, my wife, Sheila, and I went to the Globe Theatre in London, near the Thames. It is an open-air theatre dedicated to Shakespeare's plays. The play we saw, *Pericles, Prince of Tyre*, was exceptionally physical: actors swung above our heads, and words were spat out like hurled daggers. I was entranced right from the start. In the middle of this stunning performance, the narrator stopped the play to fill in what he considered we might be missing. Things were moving so fast that the break was welcome. In one brief speech before the play hurtled on, the narrator looked at the audience and, in a rich, full voice, proclaimed, 'Here [pause for effect] we do life!'

He was right, Shakespeare does life, but, for all his brilliance, he does not do it as well as Jesus of Nazareth.

What does this spectacular ordinary life mean? In Mark's gospel, we find out as he tells this story: 'Sitting across from the offering box, he [Jesus] was observing how the crowd tossed money in for the collection. Many of the rich were making large contributions. One poor widow came up and put in two small coins – a measly two cents. Jesus called his disciples over and said, "The truth is that this poor widow gave more to the collection than all the others put together. All the others gave what they'll never miss; she gave extravagantly what she couldn't afford – she gave her all"' (Mk. 12:41–4 *The Message*).

This widow's act, and Jesus' response to it, rips open the values of contemporary culture. This poor, widowed and insignificant woman, in one simple act, is challenging the assumptions of the whole Western world. Without designer labels, plasma screens and three foreign holidays a year, she is showing us how to live life. Her act is so significant that Jesus draws the disciples' attention to her. She was living the spectacular ordinary. Her life was ordinary in the sense that she was not specially gifted, but spectacular in the sense that Jesus proclaims her life worth watching. This is the spectacular ordinary life, and it is being lived right here and right now, all over the world.

So what does this spectacular ordinary life look like? It will be different for each person, as we have each been made with our own unique identity that shifts and changes throughout our journey. But there are critical areas to which we should pay special attention. These areas are right at the core of human experience, and if we live in denial of them, or concentrate too much on one or two of them, we can be sure of developing unnecessary deformities that will leave us unable to grasp the potential of our own lives. All of us are deformed in one way or another, but some of us remain so, through ignoring the critical elements of what makes up a human being who is fully alive.

What are these critical areas? Simply, they can be gathered together in the words; Father, Son, Spirit, Creation, Fall, Incarnation, Redemption, Ascension, Hope, Communion, Community, and Mission. All these themes emerge out of Christian Scripture, and orientate us towards living our lives well so we can be fully alive.

This book has been written in response to the personal, cultural and organizational chaos we are experiencing, the sheer blinding light and love of Jesus of Nazareth, and the need to bring all this together. To my knowledge nothing in this book is original, but these ideas have never been put together in the way that follows.

I would recommend that if you like reading two or more books at the same time, then reading Michael Lloyd's *Café Theology* alongside this may be of great help. *Theology for the Community of God*, by the late Stanley J. Grenz, will also be of considerable help if you want to head for deeper waters.

# Part One

# TRINITY

We begin the spectacular ordinary life with God. There is no other place to start. We have been created in the image of God, and this image is love in community. The Christian God is one, but also Father, Son and Spirit in relationship. This one reality challenges every idea we have about life and how it works, and introduces us to the spectacular ordinary life.

# Father

A panda walks into a café. He orders a sandwich, eats it, then draws a gun and fires two shots into the air.

'Why?' asks the confused waiter, as the panda makes towards the exit. The panda produces a badly-punctuated wildlife manual and tosses it over his shoulder.

'I'm a panda,' he says, at the door, 'Look it up.' The waiter turns to the relevant entry and, sure enough, finds an explanation.

'Panda: Large black-and-white, bear-like mammal, native to China. Eats, shoots and leaves.'[1]

My wife and I had the pleasure of staying in the Cumbrian town of Keswick while we attended an international conference. In a very English house, decorated in a mismatched style, we sat down to breakfast each morning, amid the rich and varied chatter of Americans, English, Canadians, Indians and South Africans. The conversation was both distracting and fascinating.

At our table we were having a polite conversation about the Keswick teapot museum, where teapots which looked like computers, goldfish bowls and one-armed bandits could be admired and bought. But while we talked a man at another table could be overheard saying,

'Rape . . . what I have been going through is a kind of rape; I have been raped three times a day over twenty years!' This loud declaration crashed into our teapot conversation, shattering the peace.

I had seen this man walking with the aid of sticks the evening we arrived, and the owner of the bed and breakfast explained that the man had been involved in an accident while driving his lorry a few years ago.

When we met him later he was friendly and ready to engage in conversation without any invitation. However, he was from north-east England and his accent was syrup-thick; his words delivered at space-shuttle speed. I have travelled the world and have frequently had to watch lips and gestures in an attempt to understand a person's speech. This man was as great a challenge as any I had yet come across and it was difficult to believe that he was from my own country. But he was very clear in his rape declaration.

Communication did not improve the next day. A couple from Essex came to the breakfast room and began a conversation with the almost incomprehensible man from South Shields. After a series of rapid sentences the man from Essex asked him to slow down because it was difficult to understand him. Instead he carried on talking at the same speed, now punctuated by short bursts of heavily accented clarity. I found the conversation both funny and increasingly bizarre. A woman at the same table asked him if he had received counselling after his accident. 'Do I have cancer?' he said.

'No,' said the woman, 'did you have counselling?'

'Am I controlling?' he said.

'No.' she replied.

Nothing more was said about counselling or cancer and they moved on to yet more complicated conversations. Later, the lady who ran the bed and breakfast explained that my South Shields friend had been listening in on our conversation while I was listening in on his. Apparently, he had no idea what I was talking about because our accents were so different! The rape declaration related to how he felt the insurance company had handled his claim for compensation.

These sort of multiple conversations are going on all the time. As the panda joke at the beginning of the chapter illustrates; simple mistakes can have far-reaching consequences. We speak expecting to be heard clearly. We listen and imagine we have fully understood the speaker. In reality, of course, that is not always the case.

So our challenge is finding ways in which we can listen well to others and to God. In the many overlapping demands of communication can we hear and comprehend? Can we ever really be fully understood by people around us? I have my doubts. We are all challenged in the area of communication. Yet there is something that God wants us to get loud and clear, and that is the intention of the Father's loving heart. But so often this message is confused in a similar way to my breakfast conversations in Cumbria.

We spend our lives living through all that flows from God as Trinity, both scratching our heads trying to work out what it means and falling down in worship and awe before Father, Son and Spirit who is God. The Father loves, designs, and is the source of all that has been revealed to us. The Scriptures teach that the Father is in relationship with Son and Spirit and through this we discover the one startling reality that 'God is Love' (1 Jn. 4:8). This means that love is the inner dynamic of God, so encountering this love is pivotal to how we live life, and live it well. It is here that we enter the immense possibilities of the spectacular ordinary life.

The spectacular ordinary life is gloriously possible because the Father loves the Son. At first glance this may seem an irrelevant statement regarding how we live our lives, but the implications are more wonderful than any experience we have encountered so far. It is here that we enter into the heart of God, which is full of love and abounding in generosity.

Scripture is very clear about this. At the baptism of Jesus the Father speaks of the Son and says, 'This is my Son, whom I love; with him I am well pleased.' (Mt. 3:17).[2] Matthew continues quoting Isaiah, 'Here is my servant whom I have chosen, the one I love, in whom I delight; I will put my Spirit on him, and he will proclaim justice to the nations' (Mt. 12:18). There is a similar affirmation of the Father's love for the Son at the transfiguration where the story continues with, 'While he was still speaking, a bright cloud enveloped them, and a voice from the cloud said, "This is my Son, whom I love; with him I am well pleased. Listen to him!"'(Mt.17:5)

## Father's Delight

The Father is delighted with the Son and because this is so, it opens up the possibility that he can be delighted with us. He can be delighted with me. This is great news. Everything we read in Christian Scripture tells us that God is looking for ways in which he can show that the love there is between Father, Son and Spirit is opened up to us.[3] God is staggeringly generous. All he does overflows from the crashing waves of love that move within the relationship of Father, Son and Spirit. The waves of God's love reach us primarily in the death and resurrection of Jesus, but are demonstrated throughout Scripture.

This love of God is right at the core of our experience of him. The Psalms draw our attention to this over and over again. 'Let them give thanks to the Lord for his unfailing love and his wonderful deeds for men' is repeated three times in Psalm 107, in verses 15, 21, and 31. 'Give thanks to the Lord, for he is good; his love endures forever. Let Israel say: "His love endures forever." Let the house of Aaron say: "His love endures forever." Let those who fear the Lord say: "His love endures forever"' (Ps. 118:1–4). Psalm 136 leads us from God's wonders in the heavens through to celebrating down-to-earth deliverance from enemies. The Psalm repeats the phrase 'His love endures forever' twenty-six times.

## Love Poured Out

After the death and resurrection of Jesus this theme continues but with greater intensity and worldwide application. Paul cannot stop talking about this love of God and the way this influences and shapes our lives if we allow it to happen. He explains that 'God has poured out his love into our hearts by the Holy Spirit' (Rom. 5:5) and now we are in a situation where nothing can take us out of that love. Paul asks the question, 'Who shall separate us from the love of Christ?' (Rom. 8:31–9) The answer is: nothing. Nothing can separate us from the love of God poured out for us.

It is in this love that our lives can be adequately 'rooted and established' and through this love we are given space to live and breathe. This is the space in which we become fully alive. In one of the most open and visionary sections of Scripture Paul says, 'I pray that out of his glorious riches he may strengthen you with power through his

Spirit in your inner being, so that Christ may dwell in your hearts through faith. And I pray that you, being rooted and established in love, may have power, together with all the saints, to grasp how wide and long and high and deep is the love of Christ, and to know this love that surpasses knowledge – that you may be filled to the measure of all the fullness of God' (Eph. 3:16–19). It is out of the nourishment brought to us through this measureless, beyond-knowledge love that we face our lives and relationships and learn to live them well.

## Evaporating Fear

This avalanche of love is intended to be the context for our occasionally trivial, and often overpowering, fears. There is no reason to live fearfully with this love of God present in our lives. John leans into this when he says, 'There is no fear in love. But perfect love drives out fear, because fear has to do with punishment. The one who fears is not made perfect in love. We love because he first loved us' (1 Jn. 4:18–19). We may well be apprehensive about a job interview or public speaking, and understandably afraid of walking out onto the street, but this is not the fear on John's mind. The fear he is speaking of is to do with the fundamental shape of our lives. Are we being shaped by our fears or by the measureless, beyond-knowledge love of God? The question is one of authority; who or what rules our lives? Is it fear or love? His answer is that the love of the Father dawns on our fears and causes them to evaporate, as early dew gives way to the warming of mid-morning sun. As the love of God works on us we are drawn into a life of love and, in the end, a love of life because our fears diminish under love's awesome power.

Jesus called us to live in this love and respond to God and others with love. Jesus said, 'Love the Lord your God with all your heart and with all your soul and with all your mind.' This is the first and greatest commandment. And the second is like it: 'Love your neighbour as yourself' (Mt. 22:37–9). The challenging radical nature of this love is truly revolutionary. Jesus said, 'Love your enemies' (Mt. 5:44) and 'love your neighbour' (Mt. 5:43) and be ready to 'lay down' your life for your friends (Jn. 15:13). It was the religious leaders, avoiding this radical love, who received the judgement of Jesus. He says to them, 'Woe to you Pharisees because . . . you neglect justice and the love of God' (Lk. 11:42) for what they loved was 'the most important seats in the synagogues' (Lk. 11:43). They loved the celebrity and fame because they loved themselves, and not God.[4]

So our journey into the spectacular ordinary life begins with love. It is the overwhelming love of God given to us by Father, Son and Spirit and demonstrated through the cross and resurrection. This is our basic grammar for understanding how life should be when it is working well.

*The spectacular ordinary life is encountering and flourishing in the love of the Father.*

*The Spectacular Ordinary Life*

## Questions and Reflections

1. Is there anything that prevents you from receiving the love of the Father? What do you intend to do about this?

2. Where is love present and absent in the funeral story in the Introduction?

3. When did you last feel the warmth and delight of the Father's love for you? What was it like?

# Son

God is passionate about forgiveness. Everything we know about God from Christian Scripture is that he desires to set people free from the power of individual and communal sin. It is a serious mistake to underestimate God's passion to forgive, for this is the thrust of all that Jesus did in coming to the world as a baby in flesh. If we misread him in this area of his passion to forgive, we may miss him entirely. We will certainly find ourselves locked into patterns of response and behaviour that corrode, and eventually destroy. It is in being made free by his forgiveness of us that we can find the strength to release others from the hurts and wrongs inflicted on us.

In January 2004 I taught a leadership course in the Canadian town of Eston, Saskatchewan. Eston is a remarkable place: a tiny town in the middle of a huge province. Staying in the town felt like being dropped onto a ship in the middle of the Pacific Ocean. But rather than being surrounded by waves and sea, I was surrounded by ice and snow. I have never been as cold in my life as I was in Eston.

I was surrounded by many warm-hearted people who dressed me up in the clothing I needed to move around the town but the cold was still overwhelming. Over a two-day period the temperature went down to -38°C and, including wind chill, down to -51°C. At that temperature the cold moves everywhere, easing into every tiny crack and gripping every object. It seeks out even the smallest chinks in clothing to attack areas of your body you believed you were protecting. It even got inside the college building, creating frost and icicles on the inside of the doors. Walking outside was like being slapped all over the body with icy water. I could not stop shivering in this open-domed freezer they called Eston. The cold was everywhere, dominant and insistent, and it took well-laid plans combined with hard work to resist it.

The desire of God to set us free and forgive is all over us like Saskatchewan cold. His love, freedom and forgiveness penetrate our outer protection, stabbing us in places where we think we have protected ourselves, and opening up vulnerabilities we never thought were there. God has a passion to forgive and will do it in any way possible. The freedom offered through forgiveness is pivotal to how we live our lives. A critical question in living a spectacular ordinary life is, 'Are you free and are you forgiven?'

## Passion to Forgive

Two powerful stories in the Bible open up the way this forgiveness works. In one story a paraplegic man is healed. Eugene Peterson in *The Message* writes

'Back in the boat, Jesus and the disciples recrossed the sea to Jesus' hometown. They were hardly out of the boat when some men carried a paraplegic on a stretcher and set him down in front of them. Jesus, impressed by their bold belief, said to the paraplegic, "Cheer up, son, I forgive your sins." Some religious scholars whispered, "Why, that's blasphemy!" Jesus knew what they were thinking, and said, "Why this gossipy whispering? Which do you think is simpler: to say, 'I forgive your sins', or, 'Get up and walk'? Well, just so it's clear that I'm the Son of Man and authorized to do either or both . . ." At this he turned to the paraplegic and said, "Get up. Take your bed and go home." And the man did it. The crowd were awestruck, amazed and pleased that God had authorized Jesus to work among them this way' (Mt. 9: 1–8).

Drawn in by physical need and in full possession of a crippling illness, this paraplegic's ordinary world was about to become spectacular. His eager encounter with Jesus brought about physical and spiritual transformation. After meeting Jesus he is whole in every sense of the word. But in this story the focus is on forgiveness of his sins, rather than the weakness of his legs. Jesus was demonstrating an important reality through this incident. He was asserting his authority over the physical and spiritual realm. He was demonstrating that through the authority vested in him he can both forgive and heal. This story makes it clear that Jesus could see into the hearts of all the people who were around him. He was also showing, in the face of religious opposition and in the cauldron of gossip, that he intends to do the work of forgiveness and healing. Jesus clearly wanted with all his heart to forgive this man, and his passion to do it overwhelmed the forces against that happening.

Another story of the passion of Jesus to forgive is found in Luke. This time it is not a man but a woman in search of forgiveness. Eugene Peterson in *The Message* writes, 'One of the Pharisees asked him over for a meal.

He went to the Pharisee's house and sat down at the dinner table. Just then a woman of the village, the town harlot, having learned that Jesus was a guest in the home of the Pharisee, came with a bottle of very expensive perfume and stood at his feet . . . Letting down her hair, she dried his feet, kissed them, and anointed them with the perfume' (Lk. 7:36–9).

After Simon the Pharisee had both judged Jesus for his lack of discernment and the woman for her lifestyle, Jesus speaks to him but looks at the woman as he speaks. He says

> "'Do you see this woman? I came to your home; you provided no water for my feet, but she rained tears on my feet and dried them with her hair. You gave me no greeting, but from the time I arrived she hasn't quit kissing my feet. You provide nothing for freshening up, but she has soothed my feet with her perfume. Impressive, isn't it? She was forgiven many, many sins, and so she is very, very grateful. If the forgiveness is minimal, the gratitude is minimal." Then he spoke to her: "I forgive your sins." That set the dinner guests talking behind his back: "Who does he think he is, forgiving sins!" He ignored them and said to the woman, "Your faith has saved you. Go in peace"' (Lk. 7:43–50).

This story is beautiful, challenging and the sort that is impossible to avoid if you want to live a spectacular ordinary life. Jesus connected with this woman through touch, eye contact and speech. He allowed her to pour very expensive perfume onto his feet and interact with him in an intimate way. How was it that an oil probably bought with money earned through having sex with men was allowed to be poured onto the body of Jesus of Nazareth, second person of the Trinity, King of Kings and Lord of Lords? How was it that he allowed a woman whose hands would have sexually satisfied many men in town to stroke the feet of the Creator of the world who is Holy God? How was it that Simon and the dinner guests missed the point of what was taking place as they slipped into offensive gossip behind the back of Jesus? Let the religious beware. Jesus focuses on this woman, demonstrates his passion for forgiveness and ignores the conversation of the religious.

These stories of Jesus interacting with a sick man at the lakeside and a prostitute at a meal demonstrate that God the Son has a passion to forgive. If we are going to live a spectacular ordinary life, allowing Jesus to forgive us is foundational.

There are similarities in these stories. Both people are forgiven in the face of judgemental religious opposition. Jesus forgives this man and woman even though other voices condemn. Similar voices can come to us from others or can be heard in the internal crush of devil-self talk that continually pulls us down.

## Faith Enough

Both of these stories have elements of faith to them. The paraplegic comes to the lakeside and wants to be healed; the woman makes it into the hostile room where she can show her devotion to Jesus. Exercising faith seems crucial if we are to live spectacular ordinary lives. It is not about 'how much' faith, for it is very difficult for us to measure it. Rather, the point is that they had enough faith to make it into the presence of Jesus. To live spectacular ordinary lives we need to find ourselves in the presence of Jesus where we can know and feel the love of the Father and the work of the Son that frees and forgives.

In both of these stories there is also a conclusion. The paraplegic is told 'Get up. Take up your bed and go home.' The prostitute is told, 'Go in peace.' Both are called to action. The response Jesus is calling from them is to go. Go home, go in peace is his message. Spectacular ordinary lives have this element of movement and momentum about them. It is as though forgiveness is only going to achieve its full potential when decisions are made on the basis of it.

In 1992 Clint Eastwood directed and starred in the award-winning movie *Unforgiven*. This is the movie in which Eastwood grows up and shows us cowboy weakness and vulnerability rather than the macho gunslinger movies of earlier times. The movie is set in the town of Big Whiskey, where some cowboys assault a prostitute with a knife leaving her permanently disfigured. Unsurprisingly, the prostitute cannot forgive them for what they have done, and recruits bounty hunters so that she can exact revenge. While watching it I spent much of my emotional energy wanting and waiting for that revenge to come. One main idea behind the movie is that we all are going to pay the price for our sin in one way or another. The prostitutes, the sadistic cowboys and the town mayor all have judgement coming: everyone is unforgiven and, even if they don't realize it, everyone is in need of mercy.

In *The Return of the Prodigal Son*, Henri J. M. Nouwen writes of the universal need for forgiveness even though we may feel no need of it. The book is an explanation of the Bible story, illustrated in Rembrandt's famous painting, of the son who wanted his father's inheritance ahead of time. After being given the inheritance the son spent his money on temporary pleasures ending up in the company of pigs. He then decided to go home and offer himself back to his father. The father lovingly accepted the son home and threw him a party celebrating his return.

Why is forgiveness so important if you want to live a spectacular ordinary life? It is because through forgiveness we find our way home. All the anxieties, addictive behaviours, fears and sins are rooted in separation from our true home; relationship with God. This does not mean if I am forgiven everything will go well for me, but it does mean that if I am not forgiven there is little chance of it ever going well with me. If a relationship with God is my true home, and I refuse to return, then all I am left with are home substitutes. Money, power, patriotism, racial superiority, sex, image, travel, social prestige, education and so on become fake homes that I can choose to inhabit. Through choosing to live with these substitutes for home – instead of the real thing – we remain shackled to our own confused agenda of what makes a really good life. Forgiveness from God sets you free, through releasing you from a self-first sinful life, and brings you to all of what home was intended to be. This is why God is so focused on forgiveness and why we can't fully live without it.

*The spectacular ordinary life is discovering freedom through forgiveness.*

**Questions and Reflections**

1. Are you living with the freedom that God's forgiveness brings to you? What could that freedom look like?

2. Where is forgiveness present and absent in the funeral story in the Introduction?

3. Who do you need to forgive? What effect do you feel your forgiveness will have on you and the person forgiven?

# Spirit

I recently visited the Emerald Queen Casino in Fife, Washington State, and for the first time observed mass gambling. The hotel and gambling complex – small by U.S. standards – was about just one thing; gaming machines. There was row upon row of slot machines where people sat transfixed by the bright, ever-moving screens that rolled out new options every couple of seconds. It looked like a hypnotic trance had taken over the complex, as thousands of buttons were pressed every few seconds. All this was accompanied by electronic sounds that bleeped away in the background as each machine ran through the symbols and numbers.

Along with many other options the punters could play Wheel of Fortune, Rich Little Piggy and Lucky Larry's Lobstermania and try their luck. All these games looked the same, their different images wrapped around the same idea of winning fast money. Even though 'the house always wins', gamblers began arriving at 10 a.m. and stayed until six in the morning the day after, before eventually going home. One Chinese woman was so gripped by the games that she played two machines at once.

There was a whiff of death about the whole thing. Human life seemed vacuumed out via the sparkling machines. It was as if Martians had taken over human minds and re-programming was taking place so the gamblers would be trained to live an alien way; as though people were being acclimatized to death through the process of taking away life. For whatever reason, they had been reduced to repetitive instant non-gratification via a machine that would in the end just take their money away. This was a substitute spectacular world where life had been replaced by addiction and glitz. It seemed a long way from the life offered to us through the vibrant work of the Holy Spirit.

## Choose Life

Men and women have their origins in two acts of God. Initially we are formed out of the 'dust of the ground'. This is phase one of our origin and it is the chemical formation of our flesh, blood, brain and bone. Phase two in what makes us alive is the breath of God. In Genesis the Lord God 'breathed into his nostrils the breath of life, and the man became a living being' (Gen. 2:7). For us to be alive both of these acts have to happen.

Later on in the biblical story God calls his people into 'life'. It is clear that a full life emerges from a relationship with God. Israel hears this clearly,

And I command you today: Love God, your God. Walk in his ways. Keep his commandments, regulations, and rules so that you will live, really live, live exuberantly, blessed by God, your God, in the land you are about to enter and possess. But I warn you: If you have a change of heart, refuse to listen obediently, and wilfully go off to serve and worship other gods, you will most certainly die. You won't last long in the land that you are crossing the Jordan to enter and

possess. I call Heaven and Earth to witness against you
today: I place before you Life and Death, Blessing and Curse.
Choose life so that you and your children will live. And love
God, your God, listening obediently to him, firmly embrac-
ing him. Oh yes, he is life itself, a long life settled on the soil
that God, your God, promised to give your ancestors,
Abraham, Isaac, and Jacob. (Deut. 30:16–20 *The Message*)

The Scripture was intended to restore life. The Psalmist
pleads with God in crying; 'preserve my life according
to your laws' (Ps. 119:156).

This theme of 'life' is continually on the lips of Jesus. He
says, 'For whoever wants to save his life will lose it, but
whoever loses his life for me will save it' (Lk. 9:24). At
another time Jesus offers life-giving bread to the disciples.
In a complex conversation around bread and life Jesus
says, 'I am the Bread of Life. The person who aligns with
me hungers no more and thirsts no more, ever.' He continues later, 'This is what my Father wants: that anyone who
sees the Son and trusts who he is and what he does and
then aligns with him will enter *real* life, *eternal* life. My part
is to put them on their feet alive and whole at the completion of time' (Jn. 6:35–40 *The Message*, my emphasis).

It is in the gospel of John where this theme is stated so
clearly. The book begins with, 'In him [Jesus] was life
and that life was the light of men' (Jn. 1:4) and goes on
to explain this 'life'.

In one particular story John helps us understand the
dimensions of this 'life'. A tired Jesus sat down by a well
in the middle of the day and ripped into the social fabric
through an encounter with a woman who had had five
husbands. The story goes

'A woman, a Samaritan, came to draw water. Jesus said,
"Would you give me a drink of water?" (His disciples had

gone to the village to buy food for lunch.) The Samaritan woman, taken aback, asked, "How come you, a Jew, are asking me, a Samaritan woman, for a drink?" (Jews in those days would not be caught dead talking to Samaritans.) Jesus answered, "If you knew the generosity of God and who I am, you would be asking *me* for a drink, and I would give you fresh, living water." The woman said, "Sir, you don't even have a bucket to draw with and this well is deep. So how are you going to get this 'living water'? Are you a better man than our ancestor Jacob, who dug this well and drank from it, he and his sons and livestock, and passed it down to us?" Jesus said, "Everyone who drinks of this water will get thirsty again and again. Anyone who drinks the water I will give will never thirst – not ever. The water I give will be an artesian spring within, gushing fountains of endless life" (Jn. 4:7–14 *The Message*, my emphasis).

Cultural boundaries were crossed when Jesus talked with a woman, but he wanted to give her life. The disciples were disturbed by his actions. This was not only a woman, but a Samaritan woman. Samaritans were outsiders and Jews certainly did not associate with them, as the woman herself pointed out. The history between them went back to 722 BC. The Samaritans held back the rebuilding of the walls of Jerusalem, as they believed that the place to worship God was on the Mountain of Gerizim and not Jerusalem. They were idol worshippers with a mixture of Jewish and pagan practices.[5]

So Jesus was tired, probably hungry, and alone, talking with a woman who was a member of the heretical Samaritans. Although his very action in speaking to her challenged cultural preconceptions, he was not engaging with an idea or a doctrine. He met a particular person, this Samaritan woman, who was by a well pulling up water at midday. She became his agenda.

This looks like a trivial non-strategic encounter but often this is the way of God. We think we know the way to live our lives but God has other ideas. He often draws our attention to something else that we think is unimportant or trivial. For Moses it was God in a burning bush, a common sight in the desert. For Elijah it was God in the gentle whisper (1 Kgs. 19:12). Jesus pointed to children – not to religious authorities – and said, 'Let the little children come to me, and do not hinder them, for the kingdom of God belongs to such as these' (Mk. 10:14). So Jesus met this woman who was a stranger, and began to show her love and life, wooing her into the kingdom of God.

Jesus had something to tell the woman about the men in her life. He says to her; 'You have had five husbands and the man you now have is not your husband' (Jn. 4:18). He gives her the gift of truth-filled words. As with Nicodemus in John 3, Jesus gives her time and answers her questions. Lovingly, he helps her with her questions about the differences between Jewish and Samarian theology and shows her the way. He explains that geography is not the centre. Where you worship God is not the point. Rather she needs to understand that the way is to worship in 'spirit and truth' (Jn. 4:24).

By his presence and through their encounter Jesus was giving her life. As they were talking she was being transformed as her life encountered his. Jesus expressed his need of water (Jn. 4:7) and explained to her that she needed living water (Jn. 4:10): the water of eternal – whole and lasting – life. He says the water that he gives is like an everlasting spring 'welling' up (Jn. 4:14).

## Free Vibrant Life

Today this is the work of the Holy Spirit. 'The Spirit gives life,' says John 6:63 and the way to live the spectacular ordinary life is to embrace what the Spirit is doing in us. The Spirit gives life by bringing the love of the Father and the work of the Son. In his take on Romans 8 in *The Message*, Eugene Peterson explains this when he translates verses 5 and 6, 'Those who think they can do it on their own end up obsessed with measuring their own moral muscle but never get around to exercising it in real life. Those who trust God's action in them find that God's Spirit is in them – living and breathing God! Obsession with self in these matters is a dead end: attention to God leads us out into the open, into a spacious, free life.' The Spirit equips, empowers and draws attention to the Son inviting us into relationship with the Trinity. From this we get Life.

The Holy Spirit comes to us as companion, friend and life-giver. He is the one who brings to us the living water promised to the Samaritan woman. He is the one who brings to us peace that is so deep it is beyond understanding and the one who fires our imaginations sparking us into creativity. The Holy Spirit is the one who transforms our hearts and thoughts.

The Holy Spirit works in many different ways, all of which reflect the rich creative nature of God who has many ways of doing or saying any one thing. Scripture celebrates a God who spoke 'through the prophets at many times and in various ways,' (Heb. 1:1) and who distributes gifts to the church as he so desires (1 Cor.12:1–11). Let me give you an example of how this works.

I recently returned from Ghana where I was speaking to leaders and pastors. It was a very rich time. Some of our most meaningful communication takes place accidentally when we don't always know what we are really saying or doing. This was the case when Diato Kouame, a pastor from the Ivory Coast, interrupted me as I was speaking to the group. He said, 'What are you doing to us? Are you teaching theology?'

I hesitated and said 'I think so, but you have to assess. What do you think is going on?'

Diato went on, 'As you are speaking I can feel my heart changing. So what are you doing to us? This has never happened to me in a theology class before.'

Then another pastor said the same thing was happening to him and others concurred. I have no doubt that this was the Holy Spirit in the room doing his work of bringing life. So for us to experience the life in all of its spectacular and ordinary dimensions it is important that we engage with the life offered to us through the Holy Spirit.

*The spectacular ordinary life is fully alive in the company of the Holy Spirit.*

## Questions and Reflections

1. Where have you tried to find life and been disappointed? Why was it so?

2. Where is there death and life in the funeral story in the Introduction?

3. Erenaeus, one of the early church fathers, explained that the glory of God is a human being fully alive. What are you like when you are fully alive?

4. How do you keep company with the Holy Spirit?

# Part Two

# STORY

The Christian Scriptures are presented in revealed, authoritative story. From Genesis to Revelation we have the unfolding of God's revelation to us regarding who he is, who we are and what is significant in the world. Engaging with this story is critical in living well and developing a spectacular ordinary life. The story of Scripture breaks down into six main parts: creation, fall, incarnation, ascension, redemption and future life. To live a spectacular ordinary life we need to enter into the story, discover its dimensions and live out the implications.

Our contemporary, empty, vacuumed-out lives are so desperate for a story to live by. This cultural deficit is exploited well by advertising.

I have just bought a pair of Dockers jeans. The label tells me that these jeans were 'Designed in SF, Cal' and explains that 'This pair of Dockers jeans is washed in authenticity.' The desire of the company is to 'make the pants that you wash, wear, hang, fold and make a part of your own history.'

So the way the jeans are designed and embroidered is to let me know that they have a history. The idea is that if I feel I don't have a history myself, I can purchase one through acquiring these jeans. They can root me into a more substantial world than the one I exist in today. The makers don't want anyone to misunderstand them at this point and go on to explain on the same label that 'the finish applied to these jeans is intentional.' The idea is that in buying them, I have bought a piece of history that will help me know myself better, or something like that.

But the illusion of authenticity falls apart when, on another label, I find the words 'Made in Cambodia' and a website to visit. For a price I am offered a pair of quality, yet run-of-the-mill jeans promising me the fake spectacular of 'authenticity' and 'history'.

I bought them anyway.

# Creation

A zookeeper came across a gorilla reading the Bible in his left hand and Darwin's *The Origin of Species* in his right. 'Why are you reading those two books?' the keeper asked. The gorilla replied 'I just wanted to know if I was my brother's keeper or my keeper's brother.'

Another way of describing this spectacular ordinary life is through the life of Rosa Louise McCauley Parks. Rosa was an ordinary black woman. She married a barber, was a tailor's assistant and the secretary of what was known as the National Association for the Advancement of Coloured People.

At that time in Montgomery, African Americans had to purchase their bus tickets at the front and then re-board the bus through a door at the back. The front section of the bus was reserved for white passengers, and black passengers sat towards the back, past a sign denoting the segregation point. As the bus filled up the driver could move this sign further back, forcing black passengers to move. Rosa Parks was arrested in Montgomery, Alabama on 1 December 1955, because she – as an African American – refused to surrender her seat to a white passenger.

After she was arrested the Women's Political Council led a one-day bus boycott. This became 381 days of bus boycott with people sharing taxis, walking and car-pooling. Rosa was fined US $10 plus $4 in court costs for her act, but eventually the Supreme Court of the United States declared segregated seating on buses to be unconstitutional. Rosa had difficulty in finding work, moved to Detroit, and struggled financially for the next eight years. One friend described this woman, who as a rule did not defy authority, by saying, 'She might ignore you, or go around you, but she would never retreat.' Rosa lived a creative, spectacular, ordinary life.

God has created the world. This is the first visible move of Father, Son and Spirit. The world is his for he is Lord and owner of creation. Therefore what he has created, all that is contained in the material world – right down at its roots – is good. Paul wrote to Timothy about people who wanted to stop other people from enjoying God's creation through eating certain foods. Paul would not let them get away with such life-denying ideas and emphatically stated, 'For everything God created is good, and nothing is to be rejected if it is received with thanksgiving' (1 Tim. 4:4). The God who loves, sets us free through forgiveness and gives us life displays his wonder and glory in the act of creation. Creation is given to us as a gift.

Scripture teaches that God speaks to us clearly through his creation, 'The heavens declare the glory of God; the skies proclaim the work of his hands. Day after day they pour forth speech; night after night they display knowledge' (Ps. 19:1–2), and also, 'For since the creation of the world God's invisible qualities – his eternal power and divine nature – have been clearly seen, being understood from what has been made, so that men are without excuse' (Rom. 1:20). God's display in creation does not fully express who he is but does give an indication of his character and ways of working.

## Creative God

God is creative in all he does. In creating us he made people in his own image. This means that right at the heart of our identity is the ability to create. He is the creator of our minds and imaginations along with the material world. Not only has God created the world and its people, he also creates today. He is bringing new life into human hearts, the possibility of which David explains in his cry, 'Create in me a pure heart' (Ps. 51:10). God is drawing humanity together, creating 'one new man out of two' (Eph. 2:11–22). God brings people from different backgrounds and puts them together so they can live life to the full. Across racial, gender and national lines God creates a people, bringing humanity to its full height in a relationship of love with Father, Son, Spirit and Church.

We have been created in a particular and personal sense, 'For you created my inmost being; you knit me together in my mother's womb. I praise you because I am fearfully and wonderfully made; your works are wonderful, I know that full well' says Psalm 139:13–14. We have been formed for the glory of God and God is moved with deep love towards those he has created. Isaiah 43 captures this so well, 'But now, this is what the Lord says – he who created you, O Jacob, he who formed you, O Israel: "Fear not, for I have redeemed you; I have summoned you by name; you are mine"' (Isaiah 43:1) and he promises to bring back to himself 'everyone who is called by my name, whom I created for my glory, whom I formed and made' (Isaiah 43:7).

Having been created we are now to live out the reason for our creation with the blood, bone, flesh, heart and mind that God has placed in us. Paul says in Ephesians 2:10, 'We are God's workmanship, created in Christ Jesus to do good works, which God prepared in advance for us to do' and this is the place where we become fully alive. The place where our personal DNA – God's workmanship in us – and the world meet is where the rich confluence of life begins to emerge. This is where the estuary becomes the sea, and the transformation takes place from river to ocean. This is where we become more fully what God intended us to be. This means we have to avoid the damaging heresy of Docetism that assumed – and assumes – that the material creation is inherently evil. God has created the material world. This is the world of the senses and to live well we have to engage with this reality, and not deny it as so many have been prone to do.

## Creative People

This is critical in our formation as humans. The way in which we are shaped is by allowing the creative life given by God to be released in and through us. This creative energy will show itself in a million different directions, but will be central in our healthy formation. Rebellion towards God closes down creativity, through cutting us off from the help of the one who made us in the first place.

We all have our ideas of the type of person whom we consider creative. The musician, the poet and the artist all come to mind. But God has gifted us all with the ability to create. No matter how dull we may consider ourselves to be, we still have that God-given ability within us. We do not create as God does, for he is able to make something out of nothing, but we have all been given the gift of inspiration. This is the ability to take the gifts given to us by God, consider where they may be used in the world and deploy them appropriately. The myth is that to do this we need to be especially gifted, when this is not the case. Often we need others to help us in our acts of creation, for much of our creativity does not function well in isolation. Frequently these other helpers are our leaders, who have the gift of bringing people together and seeing how far people can grow with some help and organization.

One obvious implication of this is that we do not belong to ourselves. We are created. One of the great myths of contemporary urban culture is that I own myself, and this means I can do whatever I want with myself. Yet, we do not own our own minds, bodies or relationships if we know that these are gifts of God to us. Knowing ourselves to be created by God radically shapes what we do with our bodies. The debates around euthanasia, abortion and our sexual practices all need to respond to the reality that we do not belong to ourselves. We cannot just do something because we merely desire to do it and expect to live our lives free from destructive consequences.

So, in the midst of our ordinary lives, full of mundane acts like cooking, changing a nappy, cleaning a drain, and delivering the post, we live life creatively. This is how God has made us, and where we become fully alive. A spectacular ordinary life creatively engages the places and spaces where God has put us today, at this moment. By allowing Scripture, community and the Holy Spirit to speak, our imaginations are fired in our response to the ordinariness of the everyday. In so doing the ordinary is transformed into the spectacular and we become Jesus-shaped.

*The spectacular ordinary life creatively engages the world.*

## Questions and Reflections

1. We have all been made in the image of God, but why did God make you?

2. What are you doing when you particularly sense God's pleasure in your life?

3. What church or group can you join that will help release your God-given creativity?

# Spectacular Ordinary Life: Alice Summers

Alice is approaching forty and a mother of three. She holds down a part-time job and is passionate about almost everything she does. She is wonderfully loving and hospitable, yet intense and committed with a very strong perfectionist streak. She also loves her husband, her children, singing, running and telling people about Jesus. One of her outstanding abilities is to face fear and do it anyway. She is also direct: a characteristic she inherited from her father.

Alice is married to Richard, a man who is her emotional opposite. He is so laid back he can sometimes appear horizontal, but he is brilliant in the way he serves the whole family, keeping them well and flourishing in all aspects of life. Together they make a great couple who love each other deeply but occasionally have their disputes.

A couple of years ago they hurt each other deeply, and both became furious with the behaviour of the other. Their anger burned into a searing silence. Richard was so angry that when Alice went to bed he took a sleeping bag downstairs to the front room. He was still furious as he tried to sleep on the sofa. Before long, though, he became aware that Alice had come and made her bed on the floor by the sofa. Richard was so irritated by this that he took his sleeping bag into the spare room. As he tried to sleep he realized that Alice had also come into the spare room and was lying next to him. He left the room again and headed off to sleep in the children's room but wherever he went his wife pursued him.

Finally, at three in the morning, she came and lay next to him again. They both burst out laughing, and began the early morning process of sorting out their problems. Alice just refused to allow him to sleep in another place in the house with unresolved anger. She was living out a spectacular love in a series of ordinary acts that had spectacular results.

# Fall

All the wonder of creation and the glory of being made in the image of God is shattered in the next big event in Scripture; 'The Fall'. The Fall was a huge act of rebellion against God's explicit will and we are now living through the consequences. This is the way I think this goes. Humanity's part in the Fall was to follow deceptive satanic powers already in rebellion. Given the choice of remaining under the rule and reign of God, we chose to leave. So the world is fallen through our sin and rebellion and this shapes every aspect of our cultures. The institutions we create, the decisions we make, the relationships we encounter, poverty, sickness and death all exist in the context of this Fall. The idea behind this is simple to explain but the implications are wide-ranging, complex and devastating. Now all of us live in various states of chaos and the wealthy middle classes of the West are as lost as the beggar on the streets of the developing world. Dislocation, disorientation and loss of identity mark us all. It's a mess.

Everything – as Eugene Petersen says – begins in a mess, and this was the case with my application for a Russian visa. The Russian Consulate in London is on a busy road at the edge of Kensington Palace Gardens, very close to Notting Hill. I have passed the building many times over the last twenty-five years but this was the first time I'd been unlucky enough to need a visa from within its walls. Thanks to delays and a laborious application process – which included obtaining a letter of invitation from within Russia – I had to both apply for and receive my visa in one working day. My friend Lloyd, lover of all things Russian, told me not to do it. I will never do it again.

I arrived outside the Consulate an hour before it opened, anticipating that while I would not be the first in the line, I would at least be in the initial group of applicants. As I approached the consulate I could see only about twenty people in front of me, so I didn't envisage any problems.

It was cold and as I stamped my feet I began to chat to the two guys behind me. They were in varying degrees of panic, as they both needed their visas today in order to fly out to Russia in the evening. One was on his way to install engineering equipment in Siberia, and the other was a ringmaster in a circus, heading for Moscow. He had only realized that he needed a visa the previous day. It was going to cost him £120 for his delay but he joked that waiting for a visa was easier than putting your head into a lion's mouth.

We carried on telling stories and sharing jokes while we waited for the visa office to open. Delighted that we were so near the front, we enjoyed a communal smugness not experienced by the people at the end of the line which was, by now, way past the bus shelter. Then the gate opened and the line moved. Within what seemed like five seconds the gate slammed shut again. Exactly five people had gone through. But surely in a few minutes another five would be released from the stone-cold street and into the warmth of the Consulate. We waited for forty-five minutes before the drama was replayed and another five were able to make it inside. Our joking ceased and we started to mutter darkly about gulags and Siberian wastelands.

Every now and then someone would come out of the Consulate and shout 'Victory!' waving their passport in the air. One person skipped down the steps like a little lamb on a Welsh hillside. It was as if they had won the lottery or had a baby, rather than just been granted a visa.

It was then that the engineer, the ringmaster and I began doing the simple maths. The Consulate is open for visa applications for three and a half hours. Only five people were able to make it inside every forty-five minutes. We would be lucky if we made it. The engineer would be particularly lucky as he had all his luggage with him and close to us was a sign warning 'Bags not allowed in the Consulate'.

As the cold took its toll on the people in the line, a Korean girl just behind us began to shiver uncontrollably. Some respite came when a cyclist who had been ignored by a motorist doing a right turn decided to chase the offending driver. To our collective delight he caught him at the next light and a great argument ensued. But the entertainment didn't last and we settled back into our frozen stupor.

After three hours the door opened and I shot through after an American MBA student. The door slammed shut on my bag-carrying engineer friend and I never saw him again. I was now inside the Consulate surrounded by many people, far more than the twenty who had been ahead of me in the line. I discovered that these forty or fifty people were the couriers. While we were waiting outside, others had been going in another gate and loading the staff down with hundreds of passports. The

courier companies charged people between £40 and £60
for this service. I was momentarily overwhelmed by
waves of frustration. The dark humour I'd felt in the line
outside was rapidly becoming anger. But if there is one
place not to show your anger it's in the Russian
Consulate when you want to get a visa. I sighed and
joined another line.

Eventually, five hours after I'd started queuing, I
received my visa from a sharp-tongued and sour-faced
lady who was nevertheless gorgeously dressed, even
down to her pearl necklace. My American MBA friend
received his visa straight after me. He was so thankful he
kissed his passport, turned to me and just kept on saying,
'My gaad, my gaad,' just before we both shouted
'Victory!' and gave each other a hug. I skipped down the
steps like a Welsh lamb and onto the London street. But
how rapidly and easily my mood had darkened throughout the day. Why was I so delighted with such a trivial
success, and why did the day feel so much like the effects
of the Fall?

## We Are All Slaves to Something

Creation – being originally good – has been shattered by
our attempt to run our own lives without God. By choice
we have thrown off what we perceive as our shackles of
obedience to God to live life on our own. But this sup-
posed freedom from a life with God has actually shackled us to our own ideas, weaknesses, prejudices and
sins. The gods we have created for ourselves have
enslaved us so successfully that we think we control
them. We believe we are free. That is surely the most
profound and widespread fallacy of all, because we are
all focused on something that we want to achieve in life,

and we are therefore followers – if not slaves – of that something. Our decision to live without God has locked us into self-imposed prison. Once incarcerated, we have then thrown away the key. How on earth did this happen?

Through a series of startling images and gripping story Genesis lets us in on what happened. It all goes back to the triangle of relationships between God, Satan and humanity. When Satan works his deception and God is ignored, Adam and Eve focus on their own need and everything begins to collapse.

Eve is reasoned, if not calculating, in her response to satanic negotiations. In Genesis 3:6 she sees that the tree from which she should not eat is 'good for food'. She anticipates that it will deal with her hunger. The tree was also 'pleasing to the eye'. It appeals to her sense of style. It was also 'desirable for gaining wisdom'. It will increase her experience of the world. How could she say no to all of that? Eve was a woman both naïve and rational at the same time. It is remarkable how these characteristics often work together. Thinking rationally does not always mean thinking wisely.

Adam, on the other hand, is passive and negligent. It is these childish characteristics that are so startling in him. He is beside his woman as she goes through her logical progression and, like a child, he passively receives and eats. This passivity seems convenient for him because now he can put the blame elsewhere when it goes wrong. Like a child handing back the puppy in January after the wonder of the Christmas gift, Adam explains to God that his problem was 'this woman you put here with me' (Gen. 3:12).

As a consequence of these decisions, fear and shame enter into humanity's experience. Both of these characteristics were an indication that the relationship with God was damaged. Fear and shame are still helpful indicators that my life with God is somehow broken down. For Adam and Eve the fear and shame were closely followed by judgement and separation. Our sense of separation or isolation can also be a clear indicator that things are not going well in our relationship with God. Fear, shame and isolation are not only personal issues that need to be dealt with. When played out in our churches, communities and nations they can have a huge impact.

The vivid reality of fear and shame are played out throughout the Old Testament. This is the story of how God seeks to love and reconnect with the world through the people of Israel. We are scuttling by at this point, but if you read the first part of the Bible yourself you can see God's response to broken people now living with the consequences of fear and shame.

We need to give these issues the appropriate weight, as they have an effect on all of us. However, often we deal with them in one of two ways, neither of which can help us. Overemphasis on the Fall can lead to an obsession with sin and failure, to such an extent that we feel devoid of the love and grace offered to us in Jesus. The other perspective is to ignore the effects of the Fall and imagine that all is fine, so long as we are kind and tolerate each other. Some of my more fundamentalist friends seem to take the first approach, while some of the more liberal take the second. But neither of these views will assist us in living a spectacular ordinary life.

I know of two major movements of God during the last thirty years that have been shattered because the leaders did not put the appropriate value on the Fall and its consequences for themselves and the people they led. They lived with a measure of denial regarding its consequences, and preferred to assert a dangerous, almost humility-free, form of triumphalism that in the end crippled them and their movements. The reality is that the consequences of the Fall can be seen all around us. Having been called to a life of communion with God, stewardship of the earth and healthy human relationships (Gen. 2) humanity slithers and stumbles down towards the dark valley floor of isolation from God. Pain, gender wars, totalitarianism, a cursed earth, a hard life, battle and death are all part of the consequences (Gen. 3:14–19). We therefore live with varying degrees of chaos depending on our gene pool, the place of our birth and the season our particular culture is experiencing during our lifetime. Our imperfections, sins and the ragged edges around our lives reveal our incompleteness. Yet, it is not only us; everything that has been created – absolutely everything – is messed up, flawed, shattered and broken. This is where we are called to live a spectacular ordinary life.

## Zone of Conflict

So what does the Fall mean for us as we seek to live a spectacular ordinary life?

We know that we have an enemy and we know we are in a battle. This is critical information in teaching us how to live. The characteristics of innocent naiveté, passivity and reason modelled to us through Adam and Eve are not going to be effective in how we deal with this enemy. Paul in his letter to the Ephesians writes, 'Finally, be strong in the Lord and in his mighty power. Put on the full armour of God so that you can take your stand against the devil's schemes. For our struggle is not against flesh and blood but against the rulers, against the authorities, against the powers of this dark world and against the forces of evil in the heavenly realms' (Eph. 6:10–12).

We live in a world of evil forces, wilful humans and our own occasionally wicked hearts. The dislocation brought about by evil, which is manifested in our own lives through fear, shame, isolation, suffering and death, is not part of God's original purpose. These things entered into the story of the world after the origin of creation. Mike Lloyd explains that 'Suffering is part of the story, not part of the set-up.'[6] But evil, suffering and death are part of our daily battle now.

In the midst of this war zone we make choices. We are constantly sowing and reaping towards our own future. Each decision we make impacts on subsequent experiences of our own lives. These decisions cascade down generations, setting up the context in which our sons and daughters will have to live.

But God wants to work with us in this battle. God does not always get what he wants but 'in all things God works for the good of those who love him,' (Rom. 8:28) seeking to deliver us from the consequences of individual and communal choices. We have an enemy, we are making choices, we are in a battle against evil forces and God is working for us and not against us. But it is a real battle and we need to face it with our eyes wide open. This means we are continually working within the mess – incomplete and approximate. This is why our perfectionist tendencies ultimately fail, making us fragile and brittle. So what if you don't have that degree; if your body is not what you wanted; if you can't afford that luxury item? This incomplete world is where God works. This is where he lives. 'A father to the fatherless, a defender of widows, is God in his holy dwelling. God sets the lonely in families, he leads forth the prisoners with singing, but the rebellious live in a sun-scorched land' (Ps. 68:5–6). God does his great work in the mess of the incomplete and approximate.

# Living on the Edge of Failure

One of the consequences of this is that we have to anticipate and engage with failure as a clear possibility, while watching to learn what God is doing through it. I would go further: we need a healthy preoccupation with failure. In industry there are companies known as Highly Reliable Organizations. They assume failure is going to happen and make provision for it. If you run a nuclear power plant you have to practise failure. If you run an accident and emergency unit you need to practise failure. This sort of thinking needs to be present in all of our assumptions around developing a spectacular ordinary life. If Paul could say, 'What a wretched man I am! Who will rescue me from this body of death?' (Rom. 7:24) it must be important for us to engage with our own fallibility and live with full awareness of the effect of the Fall. We are going to fail and that is fine, for in the battles ahead there will be failure. We live this failure before God and if we can do this it will make us wiser, stronger and ready for the next challenge.

Occasionally, I overhear my wife on the phone, exclaiming 'Oh no!', 'That's terrible!' or 'This is awful!' My imagination goes into overdrive, and I start wondering who is ill or dead. Will I need to cancel my appointments and rush off to some distant destination to respond to the crisis? Then she puts the phone down and says something like 'Tracy's cat's sick.' The drama of the conversation did not match my anticipations of the actual situation, which is much more trivial – at least to me. Our sins are not a drama to God. They may be a tragedy but they are not a drama. There are ten basic ways to sin and a thousand times ten thousand ways to receive God's grace through repentance and forgiveness.

When I look at some images of Christian leadership they often give the impression that the Fall has not happened, or, even if it has, the consequences should not be noticed in leaders' lives. One well-known American Christian leader said that Christian leadership was a 'one-shot opportunity'. He was explaining that if a leader falls into sexual sin then their leadership is over – forever. It is this sort of confusion that seems to hear the call to the holy life very clearly but is deaf to the reality of the effect of the Fall on all of us and how God can restore despite it.

The mental or spiritual health of a person or group of people can often be appraised through their response to their wounds of incompleteness and brokenness. The healthy way to respond is face down in humble submission and full anticipation of God's mercy and love; lifting you up and restoring your life. This is made possible through Jesus Christ. Through his life, the cross and resurrection Jesus has defeated all the forces of evil. We access this in humility and allow the Father to raise us up just as Jesus did after his triumph on the cross. To live a spectacular ordinary life two major responses are called for in response to the fall. They are brokenness and repentance. So

- Mess is normal. God does not make everything 'nice'.
- Perfectionist values of contemporary life just make us fragile and vulnerable to disappointment, discouragement and self-obsession.
- We will always live with the tensions of transition.
- Our particular places of dislocation can be our places of wonderful articulation or greatest pain, or both.
- We are not the centre of our own lives – Jesus is.
- We have to learn to live lives of faith and be willing to let go of our own agenda.

The key to all this is humility. Humility has to do with submitting our lives to God and allowing the conse-quences to happen. It is the most moving and exciting place to be.

*The spectacular ordinary life healthily engages brokenness and the incomplete.*

## Questions and Reflections

1. How do you deal with the messes you make, both in relationships with people, and with God?

2. What does a successful life really look like?

3. Where do you see God working for the good in the midst of the bad?

# Spectacular Ordinary Life: Peter Tarantal

I became friends with Peter in his homeland of South Africa or, to be more precise, Cape Town. Precision is important here. Location is one of the areas of the spectacular ordinary in Peter's life.

Amongst many other things Peter is the leader of a multi-racial Christian organization in South Africa. He was brought up in poverty, living his life in a Cape Town suburb.

Today Peter loves sport of most kinds and is passionate about Arsenal football club, Springbok rugby and cricket. He is married to Kathi, an American from Nebraska, and has two wonderful children, Alex and Megan. Peter is an outstanding father who dresses well and carries with him an authoritative and gentle dignity that most people cannot resist for long. He is from the so-called coloured community.

The spectacular ordinary works its way out in the qualities Peter has as a man, rather than Peter the leader, although he is a very gifted leader. Peter has been able to move from his beloved Cape Town and work in Pretoria. In the evil days of Apartheid, Pretoria was the symbolic and emotional home of white rule. It was the white man's city of government.

Even though Peter detested the thought of living in Pretoria he took it on as a challenge and has flourished through it. He did it because he really wanted to serve Jesus, and live out his life to the maximum. One of the reasons why Peter has done so well in crossing boundaries is his ability to make friends. Being generously gifted in emotional intelligence, Peter is just great at making people feel at ease, opening them up to his warmth and hospitality. He has rich networking skills, and the ability to give attention to a person in such a way that they feel special.

Peter has some of the basic virtues of the Christian faith in abundance. He has endurance and tenacity, and he can not only survive, but flourish.

# Incarnation

The third part of the story is incarnation.[7] This is the act of God becoming human in the person of Jesus Christ. The second person of the Trinity, Jesus the Son of God, has come in the flesh, 'The word became flesh and made his dwelling among us. We have seen his glory, the glory of the One and Only, who came from the Father, full of grace and truth' (Jn. 1:14). The incarnation tells us that God has come to us in the clearest way possible. He did not come to us through advice, idea or sophisticated philosophy; he came to us in flesh. On entering into the Christian story we engage with the wonder, mystery and glory of God coming in the flesh. The first chapter of Hebrews pulls much of this together: 'In the past God spoke to our forefathers through the prophets at many times and in various ways, but in these last days he has spoken to us by his Son, whom he appointed heir of all things, and through whom he made the universe' (Heb. 1:1–2). God has come in the flesh and the implications for living a spectacular ordinary life in response to this overwhelming act of love are without limit. This is particularly true when we remember that men and women are already made in the image of God before Jesus becomes God in the flesh.

Jesus walks, talks, heals, fights, argues, questions, develops, releases, resists, loves, forgives, rests, eats, drinks and prays his way through the gospels. This is Jesus in the flesh, God in the flesh affirming in the most emphatic way that creation, the earth and our bodies are good. He is also affirming that the whole of creation, the earth and the flesh are extremely important. This is a vital aspect of the good news of the gospel, for this fleshly, earthly reality is the sphere in which we live our lives. We – like Jesus – walk, talk, heal, fight, argue, ask questions, grow and eventually die. This is the world of the spectacular ordinary life.

## Wonderful Body

There have been flesh-denying movements in church history. One of the earliest Christian heresies was Docetism.[8] The followers of this movement believed that Jesus only appeared to be human but his body, brain, blood and bone were not real. They came to this conclusion because they considered everything material to be evil. If this was the case, then a God who is holy could never become material. Weakened versions of this same heresy pursue the church, sick, tired and dog-like, today. However, this dog still has bite. If you deny the reality of the flesh of Jesus other things begin to collapse. This flesh-denying idea leads to people believing that God is only interested in the non-material world.

If you allow this idea to work its way through, then only the non-material is considered spiritual. Lofty feelings, deep mystic experiences and senses of the presence of God can appear to be very spiritual but they can also confuse. Why is this so? It is because the ordinary is denied and the spectacular – having lost touch with the ordinary – becomes all-important. You end up floating, balloon-like, into a world of religious fantasy. This is the world of mere ideas, image, puffed-up ego, and endless, often pointless, speculation.

To get you back into the spectacular ordinary God has to lead you into circumstances that bring you back down to earth, taking you out of the world of ideas and lofty speculations, and confronting you with people who test you, feelings you do not want and frustrations that drive you regularly to the edge of yourself. How you respond to someone pushing ahead of you in the supermarket line will be more helpful in the development of your life with God than superficially singing a hymn or reading a Bible passage without paying attention.

It was India that helped me see the importance of this. As is often the case, it is when you look at the same old thing from another perspective that you really see it for what it is.

In 1974 I was at a Christian conference in Tumkur, India. At the end of the conference people told stories of what had happened to them through the conference. Being new to the ways of India I was not ready for the gripping and emotional tale I was about to hear. One young man stood up to make a confession. As he stood I was reasonably sure that it would be some personal reflection on anger or sexual temptation.

I was wrong. He told the story of his eating habits at the conference. He enjoyed his first meal but was emotionally crushed at what happened after it was over. He discovered that people had to wash their own plate, and that included him. The truth was that he had never, ever, been in the kitchen at home and had never done a domestic chore throughout his childhood. He was in crisis. He went on to explain that at first he just walked away and left the plate to someone else. The following day he left his plate outside the kitchen. Then he was able to put his plate in the kitchen. The final victory – and he was sobbing by now – was that he had just washed his own plate.

It was very moving but I was mystified as to why this should be a struggle. Then I discovered that all his life he had been brought up to believe that plate-washing was a menial task to be left for women. Men were to engage with the loftier world of ideas, decision-making and conversation. The specifics of the story are his, but similar ideas are often ours. India is a rich, complex and wonderful country and to understand this young man's story in full you need to understand India, but a similar sort of pattern can be seen in many places in the world. We tend to believe that the material world is less than the world of the 'spiritual' or the world of ideas. Jesus coming in the flesh denies this flesh-denying approach. This carpenter from Nazareth was not only Messiah but also a worker of wood.

## Right Here, Right Now

To live a spectacular ordinary life well you need to think and act in terms of the incarnation of Jesus. Working wood, washing plates, keeping a house clean, wiping snot from children's noses, driving buses and cleaning drains are all important human activities brought into the centre of our encounter with God because Jesus has come in the flesh.

It is the presence and participation of Jesus that characterize the incarnation. The incarnation is saying that Jesus is 'right here, right now'; he is fully here and he is fully present, ready to engage. It is being fully present and engaging in full participation that shows us the way to our own formation as healthy people.

In 1994, at South Bank University in London, I learned a very simple exercise that I often use at the beginning of a seminar or teaching session. In the exercise I offer people three words to describe themselves to the group 'right here and right now'. They can use less than three words but no more and can remain silent if they wish. The exercise is about being present in the reality of the room they have just entered, and the relationships that are about to begin. It calls the participants to notice if they have really entered into the room or if it is just their bodies. It is a call to be present. The range of words used is as vast as the human experience. Tired, motivated, eager, listening, depressed, longing, hungry and so on all seem to come up regularly, as people notice that they are now incarnated into this new experience and have to live it.

Those who live spectacular ordinary lives are present in this sense and participate fully, even though they cannot do it in exactly the way Jesus did. Healthy, integrated people are not primarily formed through abstract ideas, but through engaging with human reality and walking the walk of the ordinary life in obedience to Jesus. To influence the world around you it is best to be fully there in every possible and healthy way. To look others in the eye, to speak, to listen and to notice what is taking place all open up the possibility of shaping the world in which God has placed us. We have to look at a human face and notice what is taking place in the heart and mind of the person if we are going to be like Jesus to them, albeit in a broken and incomplete way.

Theological institutions have offered us much in engagement with thinking processes and as such are very valuable. I have benefited greatly from them and plan to continue to do so in the future. But they are only a part in the process of the formation of spectacular ordinary lives.

Books, lectures, sermons and conferences all have their part to play in our development, but without engagement with the eyes, hands, feet, sins, victories, agonies and elations of the people we are seeking to influence we will be reduced to mere rational beings, and as such be less than fully human.

*The spectacular ordinary life is fully present all the time, every day.*

## Questions and Reflections

1. Can you live one day well, without falling into dreamy nostalgia about the past or speculative fantasy regarding the future?

2. Does your body have anything to do with your walk with God? If so, what is the effect?

3. When you consider what Jesus did with his body, what do you think you should do with yours?

# Spectacular Ordinary Life: Mary Spencer

I first encountered Mary at the end of a meeting on the east coast of England. She was a new Christian, full of enthusiasm but struggling to fit into the 'nice' English church culture of which she was now a member. Mary's background was anything but 'nice'. She had been undermined by adult males within the family and lacked affection from her mother, who turned a blind eye to sexually abusive behaviour directed at Mary by her brother. Mary had sought love in different directions, engaging in numerous affairs with married men and was in a lesbian liaison when she finally discovered Jesus. At the time Mary identified herself as bisexual.

Mary was also a young woman who feared intimacy and commitment, struggling for many years with the idea of being loved permanently by God. Her choices were often guided by her runaway impulses. She rarely took herself seriously, and her low self-esteem led her to make idols of others. She was battling with all of this whilst still being very intelligent, extremely funny and personally engaging. Mary had also learned how to fight. She was – and still is today – able to battle her way through to where she needs to be. One of her gifts that she has demonstrated over and over again is identifying hypocrisy. She is able to sense a hypocrite before she comes around the corner and she can identify the hypocrite in herself very well.

In her late twenties Mary suffered a serious episode of anxiety and depression which ended in psychotherapy.

She was diagnosed as suffering from 'absent father syndrome'. However, the labelling and confirmation of what Mary already knew exacerbated her fears and she increased her smoking habit from forty to sixty per day. Mary says she didn't really begin to know the freedom of the resurrection in her life until she quit smoking when her first child was born. That was the first time she had ever done anything for anyone else that didn't have an ulterior motive and that wasn't manipulative. She says that she remembers asking God to take away the love of doing things her way. It was at this point that Mary believes she was released from an 'addiction to self', which dramatically changed her life.

She says it was as if God reordered many of her crooked thought processes overnight and performed some kind of miracle in renewing her wounded spirit. The impact of this on Mary's life was enormous, as she now found herself with many friends, something she had lacked in previous years because of her shyness in close personal relationships. She was also able to cope with the dark for the first time and to be alone without fearing what was hiding round the corner.

After another troubled time she became involved with a man who she eventually married, and they had four children. He was from India and of a different faith. The marriage has lurched like a drunken sailor from joy to pain and back again. Occasionally, the marriage looks in real trouble with her husband becoming very distant, thinking mostly of himself and finding it almost impossible to really notice or care for his wife. Tomorrow they might be back on track and doing well, the next day; who knows.

Twenty years after I first met Mary her life has moved on remarkably. The progress has been steady with three steps forward and one step back. Soon after Mary gave birth to their second child, she was hanging the washing out in the garden and says that it was while doing this ordinary activity that Jesus stood alongside her and called her to serve him full time. So, stunningly, she is now an Anglican minister with three parishes of her own. She has developed her writing and speaking gifts, and is fulfilling her call in a most spectacular way. Yet much of her life has remained the same. She still has her history, and her marriage challenges are still there, but somehow, in the middle of it all, her life is working and working really well.

# Redemption

In the middle of a very busy time in my life I looked at my computer screen and it started to swim. I stood up and walked to the door, and discovered all the strength had gone from my legs. As I have a focused approach to my own health I went home for a couple of days rest, but felt even worse at the end of it. My eyes were still swimming when I looked at a book or computer screen and my legs still had no strength. I went to the doctor and he asked if I was depressed. I said I wasn't, because emotionally and mentally I felt fine, but my body was showing signs that all was not well.

After blood tests and the usual medical routine, I was sent to see a specialist. After asking lots of questions, he told me I had Generalized Anxiety Disorder. I asked if that meant I was depressed, and he responded 'No, no, no,' in a slightly patronizing tone. He then reached into his drawer and handed me a leaflet entitled 'How to Overcome Depression'! He then told me 'Think about your lifestyle and all that you are doing, get some counselling and take these pills for six months.' In a strange way I was happy to hear that I was depressed. This was good news because it meant I did not have some life-threatening disease that I had picked up in my travels around the world.

I followed all three of his suggestions and they worked really well. I took the pills for five months and after two weeks of being on them my body returned to normal. I cut back the speed at which I was living, incorporated more rest into my schedule and I got some counselling from two very gifted counsellors. We were able to identify three things that would have helped me move into this state of Generalized Anxiety Disorder. A high-stress childhood did not help, together with the isolation of finishing off my Ph.D. and a deep disappointment in one aspect of my life when some of the things I had been praying for received a clear 'No' from God. I also expected that a friend would stand by me in a struggle only to watch him change sides at the critical moment. I was in need of redemption. Somehow I needed to find a way back to physical health so my body could be in a healthy relationship with my heart and mind.

## The Cross and Resurrection Are Pivotal

The fourth part of the story is redemption. By redemption I mean the cross and the resurrection, with all that has taken place though these pivotal events. Jesus, the second person of the Trinity, became flesh, lived his life among us, died and is now raised from the dead so that we may be redeemed and reconciled to God. Again, Eugene Peterson in *The Message* helps us to understand this in contemporary language

> How blessed is God! And what a blessing he is! He's the Father of our Master, Jesus Christ, and takes us to the high places of blessing in him. Long before he laid down earth's foundations, he had us in mind, had settled on us as the

focus of his love, to be made whole and holy by his love. Long, long ago he decided to adopt us into his family through Jesus Christ. (What pleasure he took in planning this!) He wanted us to enter into the celebration of his lavish gift-giving by the hand of his beloved Son. Because of the sacrifice of the Messiah, his blood poured out on the altar of the Cross, we're a free people – free of penalties and punishments chalked up by all our misdeeds. And not just barely free, either. *Abundantly* free! He thought of everything, provided for everything we could possibly need, letting us in on the plans he took such delight in making. He set it all out before us in Christ, a long-range plan in which everything would be brought together and summed up in him, everything in deepest heaven, everything on planet earth. It's in Christ that we find out who we are and what we are living for. Long before we first heard of Christ and got our hopes up, he had his eye on us, had designs on us for glorious living, part of the overall purpose he is working out in everything and everyone . . . All this energy issues from Christ: God raised him from death and set him on a throne in deep heaven, in charge of running the universe, everything from galaxies to governments, no name and no power exempt from his rule. And not just for the time being, but *forever*. He is in charge of it all, has the final word on everything. At the center of all this, Christ rules the church. The church, you see, is not peripheral to the world; the world is peripheral to the church. The church is Christ's body, in which he speaks and acts, by which he fills everything with his presence (Eph. 1:3–23 *The Message*, my emphasis).

Wonderful as the incarnation of Jesus is, it is not enough for us. There is more on offer from God. Christ gave 'his life as a ransom for many' (Mk. 10:45). Mark is telling us that Christ's life would terminate in an act of self-sacrifice from which many would benefit and he died on the cross to deliver us from sin and its consequences. Jesus then rises from the dead demonstrating that he is the victor over Satan, sin and death. Jesus is victor-redeemer who rips open the domain of Satan setting people free and establishing his reign.

It is only in the light of this that we are able to engage with the second part of the story, the Fall, and understand the third part of the story, the incarnation. Redemption is the delivery from bondage, the control of alien powers and all tyrannies that oppress. It is to do with freedom, release, wholeness, healing and deliverance. The delivery from demonic powers and the healing of bodies in the gospels were signs of what redemption was all about. The Christian gospel is that Life – full life – was going to come through the death and resurrection of Jesus.

What does this redemption mean for living a spectacular ordinary life right now? It means we live with death and resurrection, collapse and rebuilding, weakness followed by strength and sorrow overtaken by joy. We are thrust into a world of optimistic faith with hope for the next moment following closely behind any of the deep disappointments or tragedies we experience. But if we go the way of Jesus and head towards the spectacular ordinary life there will be multiple deaths ahead, for Jesus has died and our lives are being shaped in his image. We tend not to like this part but it is a part of real life. Relationships will change and often deteriorate; things once important are important no longer, careers once eagerly anticipated and trained for are now dull and damaging and our bodies that we trusted for so long now seem unable to respond in the way they once did. We are surrounded by all sorts of death. Primarily, we are called to die to living our own lives as if we owned them.

Jesus opens this up for us with a series of twists that are so subversive regarding how we understand life that we prefer not to look at the implications of what he said. Jesus said, 'Whoever finds his life will lose it, and whoever loses his life for my sake will find it' (Mt. 10:39). Jesus also said, 'Whoever tries to keep his life will lose it, and whoever loses his life will preserve it' (Lk. 17:33) and this was in the context of Lot's wife who chose what she imagined to be life only to end up dead. A similar idea is expressed by Jesus in his statement that in the last days we will be confronted with a world where 'many who are first will be last, and many who are last will be first' (Mt. 19:30–20:16). In other words, something that seems to promise life does not, and what looks like something dead can offer life. What appears to be first is last and what appears to be last is first. To live a spectacular ordinary life you need to notice these twists and turns and be reminded of them regularly. We need to know where there is life and death, where we need to flourish, what needs to die naturally and what needs to be put to death now.

Because of redemption we are always setting people free. This is what Jesus does. A spectacular ordinary life will be lived in bringing liberty and freedom to those we encounter. This redemptive resurrection life brought to us through Jesus enables us to be in a place of self-sacrifice, hope, liberation and empowerment.

The death and resurrection of Jesus has many implications, and the whole world swings around them. All of history is laid out here. There is the defeat of cosmic powers, the demonstration of life triumphing over death and the re-ordering of the world.

Jesus is with us in all of this and much more. He is with us in our mini deaths and with us in our glorious victories. So what does this redemption mean for us in the everyday?

## We are Fabulously Rich

We have won the lottery of life. What does wealth look and feel like to you? A yacht in the harbour at St. Tropez? Champagne in the back of a Rolls Royce while driving through Beverley Hills? A private jet taking you to where the weather is always wonderful? None of it compares to this wealth offered to us through the death and resurrection of Jesus. So what does this wealth look like when worked into a life?

It produces someone who experiences being overwhelmingly loved. All of what Jesus did through his death and resurrection was 'in accordance with the riches of God's grace that he lavished on us' (Eph. 1:7–8) so God's love towards us makes us sumptuously rich. Living in the love of God is living in authentic luxury. This love comes from God 'with all wisdom and understanding'. So God is not going to wake up one morning and change his mind. His lavish love is interwoven with understanding and given to us as a gift.

Along with this lavish love comes a clear – but everdeveloping – identity. As Paul explains, 'It's in Christ that we find out who we are and what we are living for. Long before we first heard of Christ and got our hopes up, he had his eye on us, had designs on us for glorious living, part of the overall purpose he is working out in everything and in everyone' (Eph. 1:11–12 *The Message*). There is no greater wealth than knowing who you are and being overwhelmingly loved for being yourself.

## We Face Death Surrounded By Life

The death and resurrection of Jesus may well demonstrate the way ahead for us. The way of suffering and of death is often the way of the church, for it was the way of Jesus. Grief is real, loss is real but we face these losses in the context of life. Death is surrounded by life. We face the physical death of our bodies and lesser deaths of our hopes, dreams and relationships, surrounded by resurrection.

If you are lucky, my ex-Vicar, the Venerable Michael Lawson, Archdeacon of Hampstead, will conduct your funeral. Michael does a great funeral. I was at a funeral that Michael was leading and in the silence, with the coffin at the back of the church, Michael declared 'I am the resurrection and the life'. The hairs stood up on the back of my neck.

We may have death but now, because of the death and resurrection of Jesus, we also have life. Paul says in 1 Corinthians 15:55 'Where, O death, is your victory? Where, O death, is your sting?' The big move is always from death to life and not the other way around. Bribing, pornography, paralysing money-hunger, ambition that allows us no time for anything else and destroys our relationships all bring about the reversal, moving us from life to death. Jesus is telling us that what he is doing is leading us from death to life.

This life is not only for now but also to do with the future. God is on the move so that we can be redeemed but he also has plans for the whole of creation to be transformed. Paul says, 'For God was pleased to have all his fullness dwell in him, and through him to reconcile to himself all things, whether things on earth or things in heaven, by making peace through his blood, shed on the cross' (Col. 1:19–20). It is also clear that redemption is not yet complete, although through Christ our relationship with God has been sorted out. Ephesians 4:30 explains that our full redemption has not yet taken place but we are 'sealed' by the Holy Spirit for what God is going to do in the future. This sense of anticipation is expressed by Paul again in Romans, 'The Spirit makes us sure about what we will be in the future. But now we groan silently, while we wait for God to show that we are his children' (Rom. 8:23 CEV). We live in a world of redemption and resurrection; a world full of possibility and potential. In the middle of death there is always life. Lepers, the crippled and blind people touched Jesus and he did not get their sickness – they got his life.

## Everything Can Be Redeemed

God's life attaches itself to death and will not allow it to remain dead. Vital life runs through everything submitted to God and brings about transformation. From death springs life. Death is followed by resurrection. If Jesus can go through death and rise from the dead then it means that we live in a world in which everything – absolutely everything – can be redeemed. Redemption is always possible and always available until God closes it down.

This does not mean that everything will be put back the way it was. Nor does it mean that everything will be made nice and sorted out to everyone's satisfaction. But it does mean that God can take what looks like decay, defeat and death and, through acts of love and power, send it back to its place of origin. God is always looking for redemption in everything and, in a similar way; he is always seeking to forgive. Therefore there is profound hope in all we do, create, think and build as we never know what God is going to do in any particular set of circumstances or how his Spirit is going to do his work. When Christians take the bread and wine in celebrating the death and resurrection we re-enact the truth that everything can be redeemed.

## Practise Resurrection

Resurrection is going on all the time but we do not see it. Because of what Jesus has done we live in a world full of resurrection possibility. When you live resurrection life you start to notice the difference between what will bring life and what will bring death in your own attitudes, choices and behaviours. Part of the gift of noticing death in this sense is that you know when to move on. This is one of a friend of mine's greatest gifts. He knows when he has made his contribution and when to share 'more' will mean 'less' for all concerned. He has learnt to see when death has set in and he heads for life. He lives with humility, which means an appropriate sense of his own size and contribution. He knows how to choose life.

The huge danger at this point is cynicism. Cynicism moves from life to death rather than death to life. The danger of cynicism is that it can look very close to being wisdom and even closer to being clever. But because of redemption – the death and resurrection of Jesus – we are always setting people free and not questioning their intentions while justifying ourselves. A spectacular ordinary life will be lived in bringing liberty and freedom to those we encounter. This is what Jesus did and does. This redemptive resurrection life brought to us through Jesus enables us to be in a place of self-sacrifice, hope, liberation and empowerment. This is the place of redemption.

*The spectacular ordinary life engages a world where everything can be redeemed.*

## Questions and Reflections

1. Do you take the positive and, through cynicism, turn it into something negative or destructive? If the answer is yes, why do you think you do this? What can you do about it?

2. Can you see where God has redeemed a situation or person? How did he do it?

3. Can you identify the areas in your life where you need to move from death to life?

# Spectacular Ordinary Life: Ijeoma Ajibade

Ije is a startling, vivid and rich mix of Africa and England. She is a single mother of a teenage son and works for a prestigious and well-known organization in London. Ije loves life and is happy to let anyone know that she does. She adores Jesus, and chocolate, and cherishes the dream of spending her time on hot beaches somewhere in the world. She does not like people who waste her time or have narrow thinking. She does not like anything petty. Yet, she is a great friend and inspiration for many. For Ije the relationship has to be real or hardly at all.

In some ways it is difficult to describe Ije as ordinary. She is very bright, able to process vast amounts of information and make sense of any patterns that emerge. Her brain and her mouth are always well-connected, giving her an authoritative ease in one-to-one conversation. She is a gifted writer but has not done much with the gift yet as so much else has been going on. She is always on this or that course which stimulates her head and heart: she has a ravenous hunger to learn and engage. Ije has no desire for self-promotion but her talents do it for her. Her passion to help people with HIV and AIDS, and her desire to be the best she can be at work is spectacular and yet very ordinary.

The really spectacular part of her life is the way she has taken the difficulties of life and turned them around. After the breakdown of her marriage she worked out how to live life to the full, both for herself and her son.

One of the ways she has done this is through observing her own life really well. She is able to be truthful with herself and stay constantly grounded in reality. This reality is the world of hard work, being a parent, continuous learning, open-hearted generosity and serving Jesus. Where is her spectacular ordinary life heading? It is difficult to say, but she could well be on the way to ordination as a priest.

# Ascension

The spectacular ordinary life is about experiencing the totality of God in the totality of our lives. There is no part of our lives where he is not Lord. Our bodies, our feelings, our relationships and the parts of our lives we don't even know exist are all fully known to him.

God desires that there aren't any no-entry signs or red traffic lights as he encounters us. He longs for green lights and one-way arrows through the streets of our heads and hearts. Even so, he invariably waits patiently when we walk out in front of him and display a stop sign. The way to live well as you travel with God is to take down all the stop signs and allow him total access to your life. All the areas of our lives: money, sex, power, time and place are his to shape and change as he desires. When we live our lives open to God, and in the light of the Ascension the ordinary becomes spectacular.

The Ascension is a part of Christian doctrine that does not often receive much attention. We put a lot of emphasis on Jesus coming in the flesh, dying on the cross and his resurrection. But the wonder of the Ascension is clearly important; having made it into the succinct statement of what Christians believe: The Apostles' Creed. The Creed says in reference to Jesus that, 'He ascended into heaven, and is seated at the right hand of the Father'.

Jesus gave clear indications to the disciples that his Ascension was going to happen. He said to them, 'I am going to the Father, where you can see me no longer' (Jn. 16:10). In Acts 1, Luke tells us how this happened. Jesus told the disciples that they were going to be filled with the Spirit and be sent to the ends of the earth. He was then taken from their sight. Where did he go?

Mike Lloyd explains it this way, 'His body has gone, having left the universe of space and time, and gone into the presence of God, who transcends what he has made.'[9] So after his death the body of Jesus goes through two phases. Phase one is the resurrection from the dead, and phase two is the ascension into the presence of the Father in his vindication and exaltation. This double exaltation is telling us – in as clear a language as is possible – that he is Lord over all.

Before the Ascension King David saw the events prophetically; in the huge context offered to us in Psalm 110:1 he says, 'The Lord says to my Lord: "Sit at my right hand until I make your enemies a footstool for your feet."' The whole psalm is a description of what is happening now.

After the Holy Spirit had fallen on the emerging church Peter articulated what had been going on through the death and resurrection of Jesus. Halfway through his sermon Peter says, 'Brothers, I can tell you confidently that the patriarch David died and was buried, and his tomb is here to this day. But he was a prophet and knew that God had promised him on oath that he would place one of his descendants on his throne. Seeing what was ahead, he spoke of the resurrection of the Christ, that he was not abandoned to the grave, nor did his body see decay. God has raised this

Jesus to life, and we are all witnesses of the fact. Exalted to the right hand of God, he has received from the Father the promised Holy Spirit and has poured out what you now see and hear' (Acts 2:29–33).

## What Has Happened Through the Ascension?

Jesus has sat down at the right hand of the Father. We have completion. We have a result. Hebrews 1:3 says, 'The Son is the radiance of God's glory and the exact representation of his being, sustaining all things by his powerful word. After he had provided purification for sins, he sat down at the right hand of the Majesty in heaven.' On the cross Jesus said, 'It is finished,' and now we have a demonstration of this as he takes his seat at the right hand of the Father. The work is over and something hugely significant is complete. Jesus has demonstrated his victory over decay, sin, Satan and death; over everything and everyone who would oppose him.

### Jesus in Conversation

The Ascension also means that Jesus is in conversation with the Father about us. This is such a staggering reality that we should wobble under the sheer wonder of its weight. If you have ever struggled with your identity or significance it is crucial to pay attention. This one reality, when fully lived in the life of the Holy Spirit, can transform your existence into something radically different.

Paul says, 'Who is he that condemns? Christ Jesus, who died – more than that, who was raised to life – is at the right hand of God and is also interceding for us. Who

shall separate us from the love of Christ?' (Rom. 8:34–5)
The ascended Christ is talking with the Father and we are
the subject matter of the conversation. Christ is interceding for us and mediating on our behalf for the Father's
grace and love. Paul's conclusion is that nothing can separate us from the love of God if this is happening. There
is the same idea of us being in the conversation between
Father and Son in Hebrews, 'Therefore he is able to save
completely those who come to God through him,
because he always lives to intercede for them' (Heb.
7:25). The picture is of Jesus in loving conversation with
the Father over us. We are loved and talked about in the
highest of places.

This is further developed later in the New Testament,
'My dear children, I write this to you so that you will not
sin. But if anybody does sin, we have one who speaks to
the Father in our defence – Jesus Christ, the Righteous
One' (1 Jn. 2:1). If we sin or do stupid things it is right
there in the subject matter of conversation between
Father and Son. If we perform well and people say we
are great we can celebrate the joy of appreciation, but
nothing can compare with being the point of the conversation between Father, Son and Spirit.

This completion and conversation is all taking place in
the middle of adoration and praise. Jesus has returned
home victorious and has sat down. In John's vision of the
throne in heaven he writes, 'At once I was in the Spirit, and
there before me was a throne in heaven with someone sitting on it' (Rev. 4:2). Surrounding the throne are elders and
creatures who lay their own crowns before the one sitting
on the throne and state, 'You are worthy, our Lord and
God, to receive glory and honour and power, for you created all things, and by your will they were created and
have their being' (Rev. 4:11). What does this mean for us if
we are seeking to live a spectacular ordinary life?

## Party Time

It means that everything we are emerges out of celebration. Tony Campolo wrote a book called *The Kingdom of God is a Party*[10] and in it he seeks to explain some aspects of Christian celebration. We get into this party via the Ascension. We are celebrating the victory of Jesus won by his incarnation, death and resurrection and the completion which places us right at the centre of the conversation between Father, Son and Spirit. In the book of Hebrews the Father and Son relationship is cele- brated. This is a relationship characterized by love and joy, 'But about the Son he says, "Your throne, O God, will last for ever and ever, and righteousness will be the sceptre of your kingdom. You have loved righteousness and hated wickedness; therefore God, your God, has set you above your companions by anointing you with the oil of joy"' (Heb. 1:8–9). Then there is a celebration of the Son who is anointed with the oil of joy and will eventually roll up heaven and earth like a garment but never change himself (Heb. 1:11–12). These are rich and vivid pictures of intense joy that is better than sex, food or rock and roll. Indeed, if you really want to enjoy these things, put them in the context of the celebration of the exaltation of Jesus via the Ascension.

Recently, I was at the wedding of some wonderful friends; Rachel and Phil. While they were signing the register – usually the most boring bit of the wedding from my perspective – something happened to overwhelm my heart and head. Ali Berry, the worship leader at Christ Church Fulham, started singing 'The Lord has done great things for us and we are filled with joy!' Right from Ali's first line I could hear the voice of the Spirit calling to me. My heart jumped. Completeness, love, intimacy and joy all rolled into one throughout the wedding service and Ali's song just brought it all together. The whole event was a partial insight into what is taking place in heaven. We had people in right relationship enjoying each other's company in a context of adoration and worship. It doesn't come much better than that.

Why did Jesus perform his first miracle of turning water into wine at a wedding? Celebration! He was marking out one of the central ideas of the kingdom of God and through his miracle telling us what God is like. God loves celebration. Different communities with different values celebrate in different ways. I once visited an Anglican monastery where the brothers ate meals in silence. It was a strange but compelling atmosphere. That particular day I was speaking at a conference being held there on the feast day of the Apostle Paul. To celebrate everyone was given a bottle of Stella Artois, but drank it in silence. It was wonderful.

In contrast, I once watched thick-set, half-shaven North African farmers dance their hearts out during a half night of prayer. Their music was influenced through both French and Arabic styles. I had never seen anything like it. They danced and celebrated the greatness of God who had transformed their lives and the sweat rolled like rivers down their faces.

It is here at the Ascension that another layer of our own significance starts to unfold. In the L'Oreal cosmetics advert a woman looks sensually into the camera and declares, 'Because I'm worth it'. I am sure we are all worth it but the words of Paul move us beyond cosmetics, consumerism and image. He says, 'Because of his great love for us, God, who is rich in mercy, made us alive with Christ even when we were dead in transgressions – it is by grace you have been saved. And God raised us up with Christ and seated us with him in heavenly realms in Christ Jesus' (Eph. 2:4–6). We are included in this double movement. As Jesus was raised and then exalted so we follow him. Raised from death to life and raised from earth to heaven. We are seated with him in heavenly places. We are drawn into this relationship with Father, Son and Spirit. This is the best sort of party you can ever imagine and the place of our deepest significance. We are in a place where the Lord is the centre, we are included and we have the invitation to be seated with Christ in heavenly places.

You may miss the best social occasions, never be invited to the coolest of parties, you may not be invited to Harrods of London for that VIP event, you may never make it into that golf club or that particularly cool social set but you have been invited to keep company with Father, Son and Spirit. Here is our true significance; we are keeping company with God. The Ascension means we begin to grasp how significant we truly are.

When I first became a Christian, each Sunday morning was characterized by what was called 'an open time of praise and worship'. This meant that anyone could explain what was on their hearts to God in public. There was one man who stood up regularly and praised God, often repeating the phrase 'There is a man in the glory!' As a twelve-year-old boy I had no idea what he was talking about, but that phrase is one of the most succinct statements of the doctrine of Ascension. It took me about ten years to work out what he meant. Jesus, who is God, takes on human flesh, dies and rises from the dead and is exalted to the right hand of the Father. Humanity, in the person of the exalted Christ, is represented in God. So we are completely understood. All the temptation, all the pain, all the things we do not understand are taken and understood by him. He then sustains us in his continual prayer for us. It is as we enter his family through faith that his vindication is ours and his exaltation ours. He takes human nature into the world of Father, Son and Spirit and we know that from now on, and forever, we are fully understood.

## Significant Life

Through the Ascension, everything is set up for us to live spectacularly. It is as though God has set the ball in front of us, given us the bat and said, 'Hit the ball, because now you can.' It is as though he has taught us to dance, provided the orchestra, dimmed the light and said to us 'Now dance, because you can.' We are given a world of completion and celebration – this is a world of full, rich life.

Jesus is described as being 'full of the Holy Spirit' and 'led by the Spirit' (Lk. 4:1). He lived in 'the power of the Spirit' (Lk. 4:14) and was 'anointed' by the Spirit (Lk. 4:18). He cast out demons by the 'Spirit of God' (Mt. 12:28). Jesus made it clear that after the Ascension the Spirit would come on his followers, 'I tell you the truth: It is for your good that I am going away. Unless I go away, the Counsellor [the Holy Spirit] will not come to you; but if I go, I will send him to you' (Jn. 16:7). As Jesus went, so he comes to us; in the presence of the Holy Spirit. The exaltation of Christ triggers the sending of the Holy Spirit, who in turn teaches us how to live full and lasting life.

This is the set-up. We have an ascended Jesus who has completed the work of salvation; he has drawn us into the world of celebration and has given us the most profound understanding of our own significance. He understands us thoroughly and sends to us the Holy Spirit. He has set everything up for us giving us the theatre in which to play out our talents and gifts in response to the world. In Acts 1:9–11 we have the story of the Ascension. After Jesus is taken from the disciples, two men in white appear and ask, 'Why do you stand here looking into the sky?' Maybe they were gawping and maybe not. Regardless, the message was clear. It was time to move on and face the challenges of an ascended Jesus. There was to be no more staring stupidly, open-mouthed. It was time to move on into the rest of their lives and the story of God. The incident is saying that, as yet, you have not seen anything, but go out and live your life to the full in response to what you have seen.

For us the Ascension means that now is the time to engage the world; now is the time for us to be a transforming community in our communities and neighbourhoods. The picture is of the ripple effect. The church was to move from Jerusalem – home town – to Judea – our sort of people – to Samaria – not our sort of people – to the ends of the earth – total strangers – and then on to everyone everywhere. When the Spirit came he was to lead them to the end of the earth.

What are we expecting when we pray 'Thy kingdom come?' What does that look like? It looks like the celebrating and partying people of God who are understood through, and sustained by, a rich conversation with the Father, Son and Spirit. Everything has been given to us so we can now go out into the world and live out the implications of the joyous ascended Christ. In the middle of this we anticipate this ease of transition as God speaks to us and we speak to God through Word and Spirit. This is a fantastic life! Spectacular and ordinary!

*The spectacular ordinary life is characterized by significance and celebration.*

## Questions and Reflections

1. Do you know how to celebrate? How do you do it and what causes it to happen?

2. Think of those people you consider significant. Why are they so?

3. Where do you root your own significance? What does this mean for your life?

# Spectacular Ordinary Life: Derek White

Derek is a man of wide-ranging talent. I don't think he can sing, dance or juggle, but if he could it would not surprise me. If I was ever lost up a mountain I would want Derek by my side to lead me home. In reality, though, Derek's presence would have made it very unlikely that we would have got lost in the first place.

Derek comes from the south of England, is in his mid-thirties and can do almost anything he puts his mind to. He is a fast driver who shaves in his car during the traffic jams on the way to work. He has designed and built his own house, plays cricket, knows almost everything you would want to know about computer programming, and is a fantastic husband and father of two wonderful daughters.

The outstanding thing about Derek is his intelligent stability. He tends to do what he says he is going to do, delivering quality on time. This does not mean that he will do whatever people require, but he is very willing to serve if it will help. Derek is also brilliant at moderating a conversation. He is always feeding back fact, truth and reality into any encounter. Derek has mastered the art of being reliable and interesting both at the same time for he has a wide range of interests. If you have the privilege of spending time with Derek, you begin to notice the almost total absence of self-love and ego. He is not seeking to prove himself; neither is he making less of himself than he actually is. He practises the captivating gift of humility.

You can tell much about a person by the informal names that are given to them. Several years ago I was invited to help a Christian organization find its future. This involved talking to many people and asking them direct questions about the organization they were working for. I asked one girl about the Chief Executive and jokingly she said, 'Oh! You mean Napoleon!' I later found out that 'Napoleon' was his employees' nickname for this man. He had the disturbing ability to make people cry.

Derek, too, has a nickname; 'The King', given to him by members of the youth group, and it is a designation of respect, acknowledging his contribution to their lives.

# Hope

We are all hurtling towards our own futures. The clock is ticking and we have no control over the passing of time. In some places the pace of life is slow and in others it is fast, but in both places time moves at the same rate.

My wife comes from a small town called Chilliwack, in British Columbia, and when I first visited this town I went for a walk. I arrived at a road junction with both traffic and pedestrian lights. There was nobody there apart from one older lady waiting for the pedestrian light to change to green. I looked down all four streets at the junction and there were no cars to be seen. Not one. So I decided to cross, even though the pedestrian light was on red. As I was halfway across this lady said, 'Young man, that's the way to get yourself killed!' Little did she know of the traffic-dodging I had recently been performing in London, Bombay and Calcutta.

This lady and I were passing through time at the same rate but choosing to live it at different paces, and with totally different responses. Risky and safe, dull and exciting and life and death all have different meanings according to your gene pool, culture, background, personality and the choices you make in determining how your life will unfold.

## Different Visions

There are many dreams of how the future is going to unfold and they differ wildly around the world.

Tom Holbird and I attended a remarkable conference in Tyumen, Siberia, where the temperature was between -10°C and -20°C most of the time. Anton, a Russian friend of mine and one of the leaders of the conference, was brought up by his mother to believe in a Soviet future. She had been given a vision of the future through Communism. So Anton grew up believing that the plans of President Nikita Khrushchev would deliver all that was needed, through a well-planned economy. The Soviets did have a go at building the future and you can see some of their efforts as you travel throughout the country. Russia today has hundreds of thousands of identical five-storey blocks of flats that were built as twenty-year temporary structures. The planners divided human activity into 53 segments, all of which could be performed in and around these apartments. Interestingly, sex was not one of those activities.

The idea was that, after twenty years, all the people of the Soviet Union would live in luxury, possessing their own detached houses with work and food for all. I write these particular words sitting in one of those temporary apartments right on the edge of Europe. The apartments are still here but the promised luxury is not. The hope offered via Khrushchev and the Soviet vision was at best misguided delusion and at worst evil lies.

So it was a joy to meet a church of eight hundred people in the middle of Siberia and see what they are doing to bring people hope. The talk in Moscow is that 40 per cent of Russian men and 20 per cent of Russian women are alcoholics. In the Siberian equivalent of Starbucks – and here you will have to use your imagination – there were a group of twelve-year-old girls drinking beer at ten o'clock in the morning. It was a pleasure, then, to spend time with people who had serious drug addictions and observe the hope that they did not previously possess. We were at a centre with over fifty drug addicts. Many have come to faith and ten are in training to become church planters. One man has been through the programme five times and has been free of drugs for the last four years.

## Living with Anticipation

The sixth part of the story is hope; the anticipation of a free, glorious, fulfilled and complete future life. The Christian gospel propels us towards the future, and a spectacular ordinary life is lived in the Holy Spirit and full of anticipation. Eugene Peterson in *The Message* explains Paul's ideas around the future and hope

> That's why I don't think there's any comparison between the present hard times and the coming good times. The created world itself can hardly wait for what is coming next. Everything in creation is being more or less held back. God reins it in until both creation and all the creatures are ready and can be released at the same moment into the glorious times ahead. Meanwhile, the joyful anticipation deepens. All around us we observe a pregnant creation. The difficult times of pain throughout the world are simply birth pangs. But it's not only around us; it's *within* us. The Spirit of God is arousing us within. We're also feeling the birth pangs. These sterile and barren bodies of ours are yearning for full deliverance. That is why waiting does not diminish us; any more than waiting diminishes a pregnant mother. We are enlarged in the waiting. We, of course, don't see what is

enlarging us. But the longer we wait, the larger we become, and the more joyful our expectancy (Rom. 8:18–25).

We can anticipate the redemption and renewal of our bodies, glorious freedom and completed creation. This is the future being offered to us by God. Are our hearts and heads big enough to move into this world of hope? Do we want our lives to be shaped by it?

Revelation 21 and 22 paint a vivid, earthy picture of all that is ahead. We have a 'new heaven and a new earth' (Rev. 21:1) and a river of life running through the streets of a city free from curse

> The angel showed me a river that was crystal clear, and its waters gave life. The river came from the throne where God and the Lamb were seated. Then it flowed down the middle of the city's main street. On each side of the river are trees that grow a different kind of fruit each month of the year. The fruit gives life, and the leaves are used as medicine to heal the nations. God's curse will no longer be on the people of that city. He and the Lamb will be seated there on their thrones, and its people will worship God and will see him face to face. God's name will be written on the foreheads of the people. Never again will night appear, and no one who lives there will ever need a lamp or the sun. The Lord God will be their light, and they will rule forever (Rev. 22:1-5 CEV).

At the centre of the city is God who is 'making everything new' (Rev. 21:5) with a 'Water-of-Life' river. It is a transformed, vivid, material picture of what is ahead for the church and creation.

This hope given to us by God engages the imaginations, and if we let this happen it gives us the missing link of much contemporary life; courage. We are being

seduced and intimidated into safe living. The twin ter-
rors of legal action and political correctness are creating
bland people, scared of their own gut feelings and passions. This is the devil's work. There is a fearful wimp
within us all telling us to avoid, duck and pacify in every
move we make or choose not to make. We can misname
this wimp calling it 'sensitivity' or even a 'loving atti-
tude'. It is good to be sensitive and loving but don't let
fear masquerade as either of those two precious gifts.

The leader of St. Paul's at Hammersmith, Simon
Downham, has a particular ability to engage with this
issue. He states, quite categorically and fearlessly, that 'Fear
is a sin . . . Of course it is!' We don't often think of fear as a
sin, but it is. This is not the sort of apprehension we appropriately feel when under a threat of some kind or about to
take a job interview. It is the sort of fear so rooted in our
lives that we live less than what is offered to us through
friendship with God and all he holds for us in the future.

The big picture of the future is that Jesus returns,
brings his wisdom and judgement to sin, evil and injus-
tice, and then establishes his reign in full. Satan and evil
are defeated and in a new heaven and a new earth his
kingdom will have fully come together in Christ (Eph.
1:9–10). Longings for the future are scattered throughout
popular culture, engaging artists such as Coldplay,
whose recent album *X&Y* features a song called 'Til
Kingdom Come'. So what does this longing and hope
mean for us in a world where we have to deal with
money, sex, power and time in the place where we live?

## Destroyed Death

This hope teaches us how to die. Recently, I had a real
opportunity to practically engage – yet again – with

the possibility of death. Flying internal Russian air-
lines has a certain risk attached, but it was nothing
like the drive to the airport that Tom and I experienced. Our enthusiastic, strangely Italian-looking
driver began our four hour hurtle to the airport at five
o'clock in the morning. Being driven at over one hundred miles per hour down a snowy Siberian road on
the way to Ekaterinburg Airport makes flying with
Aeroflot seem the safest and most sensible thing you
could ever do. The speed was enough to cope with,
but the sound of banging and scraping throughout the
journey managed to feed my imagination with such a
sense of danger that I sat bolt upright like a startled
rabbit for most of the journey. I was thankful to get to
the airport and – stunningly – delighted and relaxed
to embark on a journey to Moscow with a Russian air-
line.

Death is an enemy. We resist death at every turn. We
pray for the sick. We get medical help. But unless Jesus
does something very special we are all heading for the
experience. Death is not permanent but remains until
everything is finally sorted by God. A huge part of how
we live our lives is shaped by a fear of death and all the
other fears that manifest themselves out of that one
dominant fear. Psalm 89:48 says, 'What man can live and
not see death, or save himself from the power of the
grave?' and Ecclesiastes 9:3 says 'The same destiny over-
takes all'. We all know this well and it works its way
through our lives in one form or another.

Yet, when we die we die in huge hope. Job says, 'I
know that my Redeemer lives, and that in the end he
will stand upon the earth. And after my skin has been
destroyed, yet in my flesh I will see God; I myself will
see him with my own eyes – I, and not another. How my
heart yearns within me!' (Job 19:25-7) John says in

1 John 3:14, 'We know that we have passed from death to life, because we love our brothers.' One man – Jesus Christ – has defeated death. 2 Timothy 1:10 says, 'Through the appearing of our Saviour, Christ Jesus, who has destroyed death and has brought life and immortality to light through the gospel.' This was very important for Paul in 2 Corinthians 5:1–8, again from *The Message*

> We know that when these bodies of ours are taken down like tents and folded away, they will be replaced by resurrection bodies in heaven – God-made, not handmade – and we'll never have to relocate our 'tents' again. Sometimes we can hardly wait to move – and so we cry out in frustration. Compared to what's coming, living conditions around here seem like a stopover in an unfurnished shack, and we're tired of it! We've been given a glimpse of the real thing, our true home, our resurrection bodies! The Spirit of God whets our appetite by giving us a taste of what's ahead. He puts a little of heaven in our hearts so that we'll never settle for less. That's why we live with such good cheer. You won't see us drooping our heads or dragging our feet! Cramped conditions here don't get us down. They only remind us of the spacious living conditions ahead. It's what we trust in but don't yet see that keeps us going. Do you suppose a few ruts in the road or rocks in the path are going to stop us? When the time comes, we'll be plenty ready to exchange exile for homecoming.

This is one of the reasons why Mother Theresa's work with the dying of Calcutta was so powerful. She led people to a good death in recognition that it has been destroyed. One day there may be a line of unemployed undertakers.

## Big Life

In Romans 8 we get pictures of pregnancy, but, rather than a pregnant woman, it is a pregnant church. The Lord of time and space makes the church pregnant, filling her with the spirit of anticipation. Creation is also pregnant with the church and the purposes of God. Paul says, 'Creation waits in eager expectation for the sons [children] of God to be revealed' (Rom. 8:19). So, we have many pictures of huge future life. The future looks like a row of pregnant women joyful and ready to give birth. Ahead is an Atlantic wave of life rolling towards the church inviting us to surf its possibilities. This is a rich, exciting, creative and turbulent life which we are called to live now.

How we respond to this future life and hope will be central to living a spectacular ordinary life. Most Western secular models of how to live life focus on the span of one lifetime or even less. The focus is usually driven by the need for one life to 'succeed'. They tend to be highly individualized models of how we live our lives, which go no further than the next few years. This vision of the future is too small and the hope on offer is hopelessly inadequate. If your vision of the future only stretches to moving to a larger house, having more money, becoming more attractive, proving yourself to be more successful or being someone else's boss then the vision is too small. If you get these things they tend to disappoint; failing to deliver the anticipated sustenance. Houses, relationships with members of the opposite sex, image, money and work are all very important areas of life but they can never be its centre. When they become the centre a deformity often emerges. You may miss this deformity but others don't. Halitosis develops, except it's not your breath that others find difficult but the tiny, cramped trivial nature of your life. What God offers us is a huge world in which to live. God offers us palaces and mansions but we often choose to live in one room in the old dolls' house.

We are led into seeing the world as bigger than ourselves; a world of mission, social transformation, elimination of poverty and the entrance of justice. It calls us all into a world of vision and fills your imagination. Isaiah 35 always works for me. Isaiah opens up our imagination of future possibilities with these words, 'The desert and the parched land will be glad; the wilderness will rejoice and blossom . . . Then will the eyes of the blind be opened and the ears of the deaf unstopped. Then will the lame leap like a deer, and the mute tongue shout for joy. Water will gush forth in the wilderness and streams in the desert. The burning sand will become a pool, the thirsty ground bubbling springs . . . gladness and joy will overtake them, and sorrow and sighing will flee away' (Is. 35:1, 5–7, 10).

A huge question rises in front of us at this point. Are our hearts and heads big enough to move into this world of hope? Are we big enough for our own futures? This is a world where everything becomes richer, deeper and purer but remains very much a material world with Jesus at the centre.

## Courageous Living

This Christian vision of future hope also causes us to reassess success. Our success is not primarily found in our individual specific accomplishments, as we have been led to believe. The criteria of success for some of our secular brothers and sisters are for Christians a temporary stop on the journey towards our future life and fulfilled hope.

In the midst of all that God has planned for us, we are drawn up towards a future that radically shapes the present. I am growing in my respect for failure. Not sin, but failure. We have underrated the remarkable possibilities of failure. To attempt to do something wonderful and fail in the process is in itself a triumph. It is also a place of considerable learning. One of the problems for many Christians is that we don't go in for failure. In not taking the risk, we lose the joy. Appropriate failure is wonderful and to be embraced.

Again in Romans 8 Paul considers our future and the glory ahead and then says that in the middle of that future anticipation we have the Spirit helping us work it all out. His conclusion is 'victory'; the overwhelming victory of God and our participation in it is the future (Rom. 8:31–9). Courage and victory are given to us through Christ's love. Paul lists the enemies and circumstances that worked with and against him and they work in us in a similar way. He emerges with a thunderous conclusion. He lists trouble, hardship, persecution, famine, nakedness, danger, sword, death, life, angels, demons, things present, the future to come, any power, anything higher or lower, or anything in creation and then declares that none of these things will separate us from the love of God. As it was for Paul, so it is for us.

There is another vision of the future in Isaiah, 'The wolf will live with the lamb, the leopard will lie down with the goat, the calf and the lion and the yearling together; and a little child will lead them. The cow will feed with the bear, their young will lie down together, and the lion will eat straw like the ox. The infant will play near the hole of the cobra, and the young child put his hand into the viper's nest. They will neither harm nor destroy on all my holy mountain, for the earth will be full of the knowledge of the Lord as the waters cover the sea' (Is. 11:6–9).

It is a picture of the future as God imposes his will in the world and as people say 'yes' to him. A spectacular ordinary life imagines with faith the Christian future, and makes decisions rooted in this sort of hope. We have ahead of us a death-destroyed, big, fruitful and courageous life. This is the Jesus-centred life. He was the centre then and he is the centre now.

*The spectacular ordinary life imagines the future and makes decisions rooted in hope.*

## Questions and Reflections

1. When you think about the future, what do you think about the most? What does this mean for your life?

2. How do your hopes about the future shape how you spend your money and time now?

3. If there is the great hope of a new heaven and earth ahead of us, this should set us free to make faith-filled and courageous decisions now. What acts of courage are you planning?

4. Where are you ready to succeed or fail?

# Spectacular Ordinary Life: Joan Milner

Joan was married to Allen for more than fifty years. She is now widowed, having lost her husband to heart complications over three years ago. Joan comes from the generation that has had to learn new ways of living more rapidly than any of her ancestors.

The spectacular ordinary in Joan's life is seen in the way she has adapted to the challenge of continual change. She was schooled in the older values of England. Duty, modesty and faithfulness all characterize her life.

I think it is true to say that she is adored by the people who really know her. The older values of England are an inspiration, but she is much more than that. She is fully alive as she heads towards her nineties. She has survived the death of her husband and the death of her son and yet still continues to move on through her life. There have been other and lesser challenges, but she has negotiated them all with poise, dignity and oceans of love. Maybe this is why much younger people love spending time with Joan.

Pivotal in her endurance and ability to adapt have been two critical elements; her humility and her sense of humour. She has genuinely sought to learn from people whose hearts are not as big as hers. She has been able to laugh at some of the more bizarre and strange aspects of contemporary life. She has chosen to carry responsibility, and take on burdens that others would have gladly left to someone else. She is a mighty woman, and very few have had the chance to walk with the glory of her life. She is living spectacular ordinary, and has been doing it thoroughly and consistently for many years.

# Part Three

# Integration

To be able to live a spectacular ordinary life three things have to come together; communion with God, community with others and mission to the world.[11] A spectacular ordinary life is lived well when these three things form a core at the centre of our lives.

In 1984 I was working in the Punjab with a friend called Mike Wakeley. To many Pakistanis, Mike and I look much the same. We are both tall, English, wear glasses and are bald. Mike disguises his baldness better than I do but 'bald' describes us well. In reality Mike and I are very different, in both background and personality, but, at a glance, in the middle of the Punjab, on a dark night, in a sandstorm: we could be mistaken for each other.

Mike and I were working together on a number of projects, and that meant speaking at churches and various Christian organizations around Pakistan. One afternoon Mike asked me if I could go and speak that evening instead of him, at a meeting two hours drive outside Lahore. I agreed. The only potential problem was informing the people who were running the meeting that we had made the switch. In fact, they never received the message that it was Thomas instead of Wakeley, but it may not have made much difference to their plans even if they had. They needed Mike Wakeley, any Mike Wakeley.

I arrived 45 minutes late, which is bang on time if you live in Pakistan. To my surprise there were more than five hundred people gathered in this tent I had just entered. I stood at the back while someone made an announcement in Punjabi. Then I heard the words booming out of the microphone, 'Welcome, Mike Wakeley!' Someone placed a garland round my neck and walked me down to the platform accompanied by thunderous applause. I sat down on the last of a row of seven chairs.

Concerned, I whispered to the man next to me, 'I am not Mike Wakeley; I am Viv Thomas,' but it was clear that he did not want to know. So I whispered again. This time – after rolling his eyes into the top of his head – he took some action. While a man was singing a solo to the gathered crowd there was a rapid and earnest gathering of my six platform companions. My information had clearly caused a problem. While the solo continued they gesticulated wildly. All eyes were on the action on the platform and little attention was paid to the poor bereft singer.

Just as the solo finished the six men sat down and I waited for my eye-rolling friend to tell me the result of their deliberations. I was a little stunned by his next sentence. He leaned over and whispered, 'Do you mind if we call you Mike Wakeley?' I waited a moment, trying to sort out what was going on, but it was a time for a quick choice. So I said hesitatingly, 'No, I don't mind. Call me Mike Wakeley if you want.' The anxiety dissolved from his face and was replaced by a smile as broad as the Sind Desert.

I suddenly realized the opportunity opening up in front of me. For tonight, I could say whatever I wanted and Mike Wakeley would get the blame. I was free because of my doppelganger! Within twenty minutes it became clear that the reason they needed Mike Wakeley – any Mike Wakeley – was because they had a certificate of honour to present. Mike had raised some money for local re-development and this was their way of saying thank you. I stood at the appropriate time, was presented with my, sorry – Mike's – certificate, and gave a humble speech of acceptance in the Mike Wakeley way. I had saved the face of my platform companions and everyone seemed happy. After my speech and on the way home I became Viv Thomas again but for a couple of hours it was a confusing joy being Mike Wakeley. Throughout the whole experience no one knew what was going on. The platform party did not know who I was either before, during or after the meeting. The people in the tent thought they knew what was going on but really had no idea. I knew most of what was happening, but being presented with a certificate for all my work done for this community, which I had never visited before, was a very disorientating experience – particularly when people started clapping. So how can we know if we are orientated in.the right direction when seeking to live a spectacular ordinary life? The key to the whole story is bringing Communion, Community and Mission together. The challenge is to live an integrated spectacular ordinary life.

# Communion

If we want to watch birds in their stirring in the woods or in the fields, we must be awake before them. We must be prepared to be alert, alive, completely out of sleep before the first bird wakes. Indeed, before the birds are aware that morning has come. We must go into the fields or into the woods and settle there absolutely still, absolutely silent, absolutely relaxed, so that we should never stir and frighten the light sleepers which are around us, because otherwise they will make their way into the distance and fly off where we can neither hear nor see them. Birdwatching implies on the other hand this stillness, this quiet, this repose, and at the same time an intense alertness, because if you sit in the fields dreaming the undreamt dreams of your short night, all the birds will have gone long before you realize that the sun is warming your back. It is essential to be alert and alive, and at the same time still and relaxed, and this is contemplative preparation of contemplative silence; this is very difficult balance between the kind of alertness that will allow you to keep an open mind, completely free from prejudice, from expectation, to receive the impact of anything that will come your way, and at the same time this stillness that will allow you to receive the impact without

dreaming into the picture of your own presence that will
be destructive of it.

*Metropolitan Anthony, School for Prayer*[12]

Prayer is a simple process. God talks and we listen, and
reply. We talk to God and he listens and replies in turn.
Prayer is a conversation, even though it is sometimes
characterized by silence. From our side this conversation
is marked by worship, love, service and friendship with
God. From God's side he brings to us all the freedom,
love and life that is promised to his children. As we enter
into this conversation with God we are able both to be
personally enriched, and discover how our lives should
be orientated and lived well. This is what I mean by
communion, and it is right at the core of what it means
to live a spectacular ordinary life.

The book of Jonah offers up a picture of how this communion and conversation can work. If you have my sense
of humour, this wonderful and short book is very funny.
The high stakes, Jonah's bungling, the scared but loyal
sailors, God's patience and the big fish all go into the mix of
prayer and obedience. Briefly, God wants Jonah to do some
work for him in Nineveh, Jonah resists and runs but God is
ahead of Jonah – as he always is – and brings him to a place
of submission through the strategic use of a big fish. Jonah
decides to obey, God moves his agenda on without con-
sulting Jonah, so he pouts and whines, 'I am angry enough
to die' (Jn. 4:9). God teaches Jonah a lesson and explains his
compassion for Nineveh. In the middle of this continual
interaction and conversation with God Jonah prays

Then Jonah prayed to the Lord his God from the belly of the
   fish, saying,
'I called to the Lord out of my distress,
 and he answered me;

out of the belly of Sheol I cried,
 and you heard my voice.
You cast me into the deep,
 into the heart of the seas,
 and the flood surrounded me;
all your waves and your billows
 passed over me.
Then I said, "I am driven away
 from your sight;
how shall I look again
 upon your holy temple?"
The waters closed in over me;
 the deep surrounded me;
weeds were wrapped around my head
 at the roots of the mountains.
I went down to the land
 whose bars closed upon me for ever;
yet you brought up my life from the Pit,
 O Lord my God.
As my life was ebbing away,
 I remembered the Lord;
and my prayer came to you,
 into your holy temple.
Those who worship vain idols
 forsake their true loyalty.
But I with the voice of thanksgiving
 will sacrifice to you;
what I have vowed I will pay.
 Deliverance belongs to the Lord!'
Then the Lord spoke to the fish, and it spewed Jonah out
 upon the dry land.

(Jn. 2:1–10 NRSV)

Jonah was in communion with God in the midst of the
most extreme circumstances. He acknowledged that

God was in charge, he prayed using all the images that surrounded him and ended with thanksgiving and deliverance. Then with one move of the fish's gut he was spewed out into his future. That is great prayer.

For the development of a spectacular ordinary life this area of communion and conversation with God is critical. The nature of our conversation with God will determine much of our response to ourselves and the world. So the more I can pray in my *real* life the better. This is what the Psalms celebrate.

Eugene Peterson in one of his more prophetic and radical statements regarding prayer has said, 'Abstraction is an enemy to prayer. Beautiful ideas are an enemy to prayer. Fine thoughts are an enemy to prayer. Authentic prayer begins when we stub our toes on a rock, get drenched in a rainstorm, get slapped in the face by an enemy – or run into a tree that has been in our path for so long that we have ceased to see it, and now stand back, in bruised and wondering awe before it.'[13] Peterson is calling for us to bring the whole of our lives into conversation with God and pray *real*.

Scripture is central to this process of communion. For a spectacular ordinary life to be formed well we need to engage with Scripture, as this is how we encounter God through the revelation of the Holy Spirit. There needs to be a continual engagement with the disciplines of exegesis and hermeneutics, so that we just do not fill the holy text with our own meaning and trample all over divine revelation. But we also need to meditate on Scripture so that our spirits are inspired and hearts fed. Both head and heart need to be engaged in our listening to God through Scripture. To live a spectacular ordinary life Word and Spirit need to come together, forming us and gathering up all of our intellect, feeling, relationships and flesh before thrusting us out into the world.

Ghana is a colourful and delightfully intense country. The impact of the church on the life of Ghana is huge. The language of Scripture has hit the streets in a remarkable way. As you drive around Kumasi or Accra you see some startling billboards and business names. There is the Holy Ghost Telephone Company, and the Jesus is Lord Beauty Parlour; with pictures of beautiful women plastered around the front of the shop. But my favourite is the Only God Knows Engineering Entity. The title of the company sounds like the final line in the contract for when things go wrong.

The point is that the language of God-encounter is not just in the churches but on the streets. Church and street have come together echoing truth from one to the other. In many ways the church has moved into the street and the street into the church. This was and is the continual challenge. How can God-encounter be in the church and in the street? This is the vision given to us in the Hebrew Scriptures and Daniel helps us enter into the potential offered.

Daniel, a very gifted man, was in exile in Babylon but still managed to work out his life with God. Much of what he was comes together in Daniel 6. What do we learn from Daniel as he communed with God, while he headed for the lions and lived under the pressure of near-death encounter?

## Communion is Conversation with God

The intention of Daniel's heart was to live for God, and he directed his energy towards this. He entered into continual conversation with God (Dan. 6:10). He talked to God in times of pressure, God gave him startling revelations, and Daniel was sustained through that conversation even though many things happened that he did not like or understand. Daniel helps us to grasp how prayer works. But how we pray and how Daniel prayed does not get to the centre of communion with God. There are two core realities that will shape everything we understand about communion with God and help develop a spectacular ordinary life.

We are not the centre of our prayer lives; Jesus is.

The Scripture says, 'Jesus lives for ever, he has a permanent priesthood. Therefore he is able to save completely those who come to God through him, because he always lives to intercede for them' (Heb. 7:24–5). We are not the centre, nor the sustainers of our own prayer lives; Jesus is. We are sustained in prayer by Jesus' prayers for us, the work that Jesus has already accomplished on the cross and through the resurrection. Jesus has done the work and now we rest on and live in the freedom given to us. We pray but the experience is like being a mouse on the back of an elephant. Jesus is the elephant and we are the mouse. He carries us, not the other way around.

We meddle with this order at our peril, but meddle we do. The meddling shows itself in our belief that we sustain our own prayer lives. Consumed by our own passions, visions, emptiness, desperation and arrogance we assume that the centre of our prayer lives is our work in making it happen. When caught up in our own agendas – even though they may be religious agendas – we go through a shift that turns prayer into a powerful tool to deliver answers to our own burdens, rather than an encounter of release and freedom offered to us through Jesus Christ. It is important we pray out our passions and visions. Prayer does work. But the point of prayer is not what prayer delivers. The core of prayer is the development of a loving, healthy and full relationship with Father, Son and Spirit that produces a great life that does 'work'.

### The Holy Spirit provides the language and power in prayer

Not only is Jesus the centre but the Holy Spirit is there too, giving us language in prayer. 'In the same way, the Spirit helps us in our weakness. We do not know what we ought to pray for, but the Spirit himself intercedes for us with groans that words cannot express. And he who searches our hearts knows the mind of the Spirit, because the Spirit intercedes for the saints in accordance with God's will' (Rom. 8:26–7). Unable to fully know ourselves, and coming from a place of inadequacy, we depend on the work of the Holy Spirit for communion with God. The Holy Spirit fully understands us, and fully understands God, and wonderfully gives us a language for communion with God. Central to living a spectacular ordinary life is listening to and living with the Holy Spirit.

So this life of the Trinity is the place of prayer. We commune with Father, Son and Holy Spirit. This is our country, these are our friends, this is the land of relationship with God. Prayer at its core is the easiest thing in the world. It is a place of rest, dependence, rich friendship and luxurious living for the heart. Of course there are further complexities when it comes to intercessory battles and ways of contemplation, but if these more developed engagements are not earthed in the sheer joy of a free, loving, dependent relationship with Father, Son and Spirit then they often collapse into self-indulgence, addictive behaviour and pride.

## Communion Happens in a Place

These days I am often on the London Underground travelling on the District, Circle or Piccadilly line. My journeys almost always include Victoria station. At Victoria while you wait for the train you hear frequent announcements; 'Stand back, a train is approaching', 'Mind the gap', 'Please let the passengers off the train first' and so on.

But recently there was one man who did these announcements differently. He was clearly inspired either by a visit to EuroDisney or Alton Towers. I can't quote him exactly but he began with something like, 'Welcome to Victoria station, I hope you have a good day, soon your train will be coming to speed you off to your destination. Today we are going to give you a good ride!' As the train approached he blessed us with, 'Your train will soon be here – have a great day'. As we were waiting for the train to depart, he declared 'Please mind the closing doors – your ride is now ready to rumble!'

To him this was not the London Underground; it was something else. His imagination was working with another set of ideas and these ideas made the train an exciting fairground ride, transforming the passengers who just needed to get from A to B into customers about to go through a positive and thrilling experience. For me, and probably many others, ordinary Victoria station was transformed.

Daniel had to live in Babylon; there was no other place available. So Daniel put himself into the way of God in the place where he lived. He had to live with its streets, buildings, tastes and fashions. He had to interact with its smells, noise, frustrations, wicked people and possibilities. Daniel can help us here. This is very important for us, because one of the mistakes the church has made over the years is to dream of some Utopia where everything will be wonderful. We ache to be somewhere else, doing really great things, living a free and full life. Some of our fantasies reveal our reluctance to pray in the place God has put us:

> 'If only we could just be like the early church.'
> 'If only we could just be like the church in Korea.'
> 'If only I could live in the country.'

All prayer is rooted in a particular place and does not inhabit 'sublime truths' or 'lofty thoughts'. Eugene Peterson explains, 'Theology separated from geography gets us into nothing but trouble.'[14] And the trouble is that if we do not acknowledge and accept where we are, and who we are, we tend to marginalize prayer, making it into a sweet, lovely experience that remains irrelevant to the strife of the world and the guts of our lives. Prayer is not for super-spiritual elites who have special knowledge or revelations. There are no experts in prayer.

The way to pray in London is not to avoid it but to notice it, giving its geography and its people your full attention. Daniel prays well in Babylon because it has his attention. He does not avoid Babylon; he heads for it, turning into the huge waves it offers and seeing what God will do amid the chaos and personal threat.

Daniel had to encounter the enemies of Babylon. His world, like ours, was not always a nice place. Much of what we encounter is in battle of one sort or another. The continual battle of the world, the flesh and the Devil is constant. Enemies of various types are ranged against us. Daniel's enemies sought to trip, trap and kill him. But Daniel prayed. Daniel lived a trustworthy and diligent life and his enemies hated him for it. They hated him and he prayed.

Yet there is another aspect to this. Daniel fully lived and prayed in Babylon but his attention was on another city that was wholly inspirational. Jerusalem was his primary context for dealing with Babylon. When he prayed he looked towards Jerusalem. He engaged Babylon through Jerusalem. He was able to live and pray well in Babylon because his imagination was fired by Jerusalem. Jerusalem was his true home. It was the city of God – the picture of what a city should be, filled with life and filled with God. In a similar way we can live and pray well in our towns and cities because we live in present reality and anticipation of the coming of the Kingdom of God. This does not distract us from the places where we live but opens up a way of praying and serving in a full way. Get a vision for the kingdom of God and it will teach you how to live and pray well in the place where you live.

## Communion Moves in Rhythm

Daniel developed habits of prayer. He went into his home, walked upstairs, opened his windows, got on his knees and prayed towards Jerusalem three times a day (Dan. 6:13). He was in a rhythm that even the threat of death could not break. If we are going to commune with God we need to develop rhythm and we need to practise. We are going to need consistent rhythmic immersion into conversation with God. Our great urban centres run on adrenaline with continual stimulation of the senses. This is one of the things I love about London. It is rare for me to move around London without a sense of stimulation and possibility. Anything could and probably will happen in London. But an addiction to immediate sensation can seriously damage your communion with God.

We live our lives with rhythm. We live with the change of seasons, day and night, breathing in and out, work and sleep and the regular beat of our hearts. To carry the weight of the place where we live we need to develop strong shoulders and necks that are able to bear the responsibility of its transformation. This strength comes through sustained and rhythmic practised prayer.

All of us have some decisions to make at this point. The way we think life goes is that, 'I believe, then I behave' or 'I feel, then I act'. So my will and my feelings come first. This is the way I have been brought up. It is convenient in that it begins with me and keeps my sense of self intact. It is deadly in that it casts me as a little lord of my little life and prevents me from flourishing beyond my own experience. But there is another way of doing this. Instead of thinking or feeling my way into new ways of behaving, I behave my way into new ways of believing. In other words I put my head, heart and hands into a rhythm of practices that will shape me. So if we are going to pray rhythmically in participation with Father, Son and Spirit, it will look something like Richard Foster's outline in his very helpful book *Celebration of Discipline*. He talks of

The inward disciplines

Meditation
Prayer
Fasting
Study

The outward disciplines

Simplicity
Solitude

Submission
Service

The communal disciplines

Confession
Worship
Guidance
Celebration

Practising all of these disciplines opens up the way for us to live rhythmically, and therefore to live well. Much of our communion with God is developed through this routine. As Christine Pohl says, 'While we might imagine sacrifice in terms of one moment of heroic martyrdom, faithful hospitality usually involves laying our lives down in little pieces, in small acts of sacrificial love and service'[15] and so it is in our communion with God.

*The spectacular ordinary life flourishes in intimacy with God.*

## Questions and Reflections

1. Is your prayer life a joy or just work? What does it mean if prayer is a chore?

2. Why do so many Christians feel inadequate when it comes to prayer and communion with God? What could be the cause of this, and how can it be changed?

3. Do you think God likes you? What difference does it make if he does or does not?

# Spectacular Ordinary Life: Ann Dacca

Ann is from Scotland, married and in her mid-forties. She comes from a solid conservative Christian family and as a child went to church regularly. She has always been quick-witted, eloquent and an analytical thinker but this has been textured into a rich and fun-loving personality that is always ready to engage with people and their varied stories. She is always ready to dance even though she never had the chance to do so as a child. She would describe herself as 'ordinary' and says things like, 'I am not a visionary' but she is not as ordinary as she thinks and has more vision than she supposes.

One of the outstanding characteristics of her life is friendship. Ann is great company and able to make friends with all sorts of people. Her friends enjoy her company and respect her for her loyalty, love and honesty. She has a deep desire to be generous and just loves giving money away. Being totally disenchanted by a culture of celebrity in any sphere, she is passionate that people who are perceived as weaker or voiceless need to be heard.

The spectacular side of her life relates to the way she has flourished into maturity. Ann has just opened up over the last six years. She has always been a first-class administrator but has always avoided counselling or helping people with their innermost feelings. It was not that she ran away, rather that she remained uninvolved, unless it was a close friend. One particular breakthrough came for Ann in relationship to her father. She had always struggled to accept him and felt instead that her father loved her but did not necessarily like her. Her father gave her money but not much time or appropriate loving attention.

The most spectacular thing that happened to Ann related to how she read the Bible. As a child she had been schooled in a factual and propositional relationship to the Bible. It was a book of good and worthy ideas about a God in whom she believed. But everything changed when she started to read the Bible contemplatively rather than factually. In her words, 'It was like a new faith'. One huge revelation for her was that she realized she saw God as she saw her earthly father. Through a contemplative reading of Scripture and keeping company with the Holy Spirit Ann has been changed. Now the focus of her life is on bringing people into rich, powerful and loving encounters with God. She is deeply appreciated by those who have the privilege of spending time with her. Ann is living spectacular ordinary and is heading into her most effective years as a Christian leader.

# Community

I arrived in India in 1976, full of curiosity and passion. India did not disappoint me then and it never has since. I have had two life-saving operations in India, one in Rajasthan in 1977 and another in Hyderabad in 1999, so I owe a lot to India and its people.

One of the things I enjoy most in India is watching men relate. You can see fully-developed masculinity being played out free of the fear of self-revelation or intimacy that plagues so many Westerners. India has its problems like the rest of the world but it – like other parts of Asia – has much to teach us regarding how relationships and community work.

God works everything out of relationship. Right at the heart of the universe is a relationship of love between Father, Son and Spirit. Each of us is made in this Trinitarian communal image. So it follows that relationship and community become foundational to all we are, decide, think and do. When we are not in community we are lost. We become like space-walking astronauts who have had the cord cut by some evil genius in the mothership. We float off into profound loneliness, losing touch with home and facing eventual death. Even our expensively designed space suits and brilliant technology do not save us when the cord is cut. The irony is that many of us are our own evil genius cutting ourselves off from the mothership and pushing ourselves off into deep space. Isolation and loneliness characterize much of the technologically-advanced world.

We have been created as communal beings, although in healthy communities we always retain our own individuality. We are formed in communities, shaped, fed, challenged and occasionally damaged by them. It is the breakdown in community in the West that makes Western models of living – even the Christian ones – so fragile and alienating even though they may appear to be effective and efficient. As the Xhosa people say, 'Persons depend on other persons to be persons' (umuntu ngumuntu ngabantu). One of the critical needs in developing a spectacular ordinary life is developing a mentored life, a life lived with others. Our lives need to be shaped, protected and released by others who have been these ways before. You only get that in community. So much of life in our cities is characterized by financial and technological wealth but relational poverty. This is one of the greatest challenges we face.

## Early Church, Spectacular Ordinary

Much can happen in eighteen months and it did when Paul was in Corinth. In Acts 18 we have the themes of money, friendship, persecution, abuse, fear, difficult decision-making, people coming to faith, people hating other people, politics, religion and a man getting beaten up for no apparent reason. In short, we have the day-to-day stuff of our urban lives.

In the first century world Athens was the political capital, Corinth the commercial capital and Ephesus the commercial and religious centre. Corinth had a temple to Aphrodite and one thousand prostitutes that worked the city based around the temple. It was the home of sexual immorality.

Paul came to Corinth and stayed with a married couple called Priscilla and Aquila. They were refugees who had just been thrown out of Rome, probably because of persecution by Claudius. When he arrived, Paul was broke so he worked with Priscilla and Aquila as a tentmaker or leatherworker. Every Sabbath he went to the Synagogue and explained Christ to the Jews and Greeks.

After some time Silas and Timothy arrived with a financial gift from Philippi so Paul stopped his leatherwork and focused on preaching the gospel. It was a battle. Paul encountered great opposition and, in some considerable emotion, he declared that he was not responsible for the Jews and headed off next door to the Gentiles. This was a very successful move because Crispus, the synagogue ruler, and many Corinthians came to faith and were baptized. In the midst of all this turmoil, in the dead of night, God spoke to Paul in a significant dream encouraging him. The dream seemed to be to do with Paul's fear. Sometime during his stay in Corinth the Jews who had rejected Paul made a specific attack on him saying that what he was teaching was against their laws. Just as Paul was about to open his mouth and defend himself, Gallio, the proconsul of Achaia, interrupted him. Gallio told the Jews that their accusations against Paul were insignificant and threw them out. The energy of their anger had to go somewhere so they turned on the unfortunate Sosthenes and beat him up. This sounds like an average Saturday night in central London to me: spectacular and ordinary.

This story and the book of Acts challenge some myths about how life works. Myths like

If I serve God everything will be smooth and problem free
If I serve God I will always be happy and have pleasant
    feelings
If I serve God I can control my life and always know what
    is going on
If I serve God through thinking well all will be fine.

We are drawn into real church, both spectacular and ordinary. The book of Acts shows us how the church actually worked, rather than just looking at the gloss we often cover it with. So how did this church work and become established?

## Dynamic Flexible Community

The way in which God's work is done is always through community of some sort or another. This should not be surprising as God himself is a community of Father, Son and Spirit. The way he works reflects his own reality.

Paul had new friends in Priscilla and Aquila; they show him love and hospitality, sharing their life with him. Old friends in the shape of Silas and Timothy come and work with Paul in Corinth. Distant friends help finance the whole project with gifts from the church in Philippi.[16] All of these relationships are practical, involved and dependent. They also prove to be effective. God's work is built on such dynamic communities.

In these communities, neighbourliness and mere acquaintance won't cut it. These older English, mostly middle-class virtues are very helpful introductions to friendship but they will not do to facilitate culture-transforming communities. Can you imagine these values being played out through Scripture?

When Meshach, Shadrach and Abednego say to Nebuchadnezzar in Daniel 3 that they will not worship the image he set up and are about to be thrown into the fiery furnace, are they friends with deep-lasting, death-challenging relationships or neighbours who chat over the garden fence and have an occasional drink?

When some of David's men risk their lives in 1 Chronicles 11 because they love and want to serve David, what is really going on? Are they neighbours or have they become a culture-transforming community? David expresses a desire for a drink of the water from Bethlehem and they risk their lives to get it. Are they living substantial, integrated relationships or just being neighbourly?

In the upper room when Jesus washed the disciples' feet, were they neighbours and acquaintances, or was something going on that was much deeper?

When Paul and Silas were in prison together after they'd had their clothes ripped off and been beaten black and blue, they were praying and singing at midnight. Were they merely neighbours or acquaintances at this point? I don't think they were talking about the condition of their lawns or their recent holiday in Cyprus. They were bound together in one community under the rule and reign of Jesus; they were death-defying friends.


## Turbulent Emotional Community

There is raw emotion in the middle of this community. Paul explained that 'When I came to you, brothers, I did not come with eloquence or superior wisdom as I proclaimed to you the testimony about God. For I resolved to know nothing while I was with you except Jesus Christ and him crucified. I came to you in weakness and fear, and with much trembling' (1 Cor. 2:1–3) or as *The Message* explains it, he felt 'totally inadequate' and 'scared to death'. Some of the Jews opposed Paul and he walked out saying 'Your blood be on your own heads!' and moved the action to next door. He shook the dust off his clothes as a clear symbolic rejection of them. When Paul's words and works were rejected he was afraid and exasperated, yet he still engaged in the work of God. In the turbulence of the emotional, cultural and physical challenge he kept on doing what God wanted him to do.

How fragile can we be by comparison? We can be so aware of our own feelings and sensibilities that we just become indulgent and soft, unable to see the debilitating effect of our indecisions on our cotton-wool lives. Healthy community is forged in raw emotion and strong feeling, not in fogs of niceness that confuse every issue and blur all sharp edges.

## Open Community

God spoke to Paul in a dream. It was clearly important to Paul and helped in sustaining his eighteen months of work in Corinth. Through the dream he hears:

Do not be afraid
Keep speaking
Do not be silent
I am with you
No one is going to harm you

Paul was exasperated and 'scared to death' but God spoke to him. It is vital that we hear the word of God at the right time, in whatever way the Holy Spirit speaks. Of course, we need to be watchful. Not all dreams or visions come from God. We need to assess all of our experiences in the light of scriptural revelation and see what God is saying through them. But after that, what can this sort of dream and vision do for you? It does what it did for Paul. It reorganizes reality and explains the context in which you are working. Part of our task as disciples is to be ready for God's surprises. God was speaking directly to Paul in this situation as well as building dynamic community in conditions of emotional turbulence: spectacular ordinary indeed.

## Community Out of Control

Life is unpredictable. In the book of Acts massive transitions were taking place from synagogue to home, and from Jew to Gentile, but if you read this story in the wrong way you would come up with the wrong conclusion. Much of the way in which the Life of God was spreading throughout the world was in the small, almost incidental stuff that seemed insignificant at the time.

Our contemporary culture tells us that we need to be in control. If things are not going well the general idea is that we watch a television programme or read a magazine that will teach us how to have a house, body or life makeover that will help us regain control. Get educated, look better, discover spirituality and influential company and then everything will work out well. This culture calls us to live strategic and sorted lives; far away from how life really works.

The spectacular ordinary life is dependent on the ability to live without needing to addictively grab the controls. For the emerging Christian community in Corinth it was their ability to flex and swerve in response to the conditions they were living through that enabled them to flourish. Paul had to sustain an unpredicted and 'united attack' (Acts 18:12). Just as Paul was about to defend himself, God intervenes, through Gallio, a local leader, so that Paul does not say a word (Acts 18:14) and in the end, one of the church leaders is beaten up. Paul and the church could not predict or control any of these events. Gallio's decision to back Paul and the gospel was decisive. It opened up the world to the gospel. This fight with the Jews was a fight Paul would not have wanted, but it was crucial for the gospel in its transition out of one group and into the rest of the world.

Paul had a passion for adoring and explaining Jesus; he had the big stuff right. What he could not control were the day-to-day events: the so-called small stuff of his life. Yet this small stuff is important, not only for itself but also for the big strategic shifts. It is often through turbulence, personal attacks and the disruption of plans that God does much of his work, because sometimes failure is the only way God can show us who is really in control.

Mine and Sheila's twenty-eighth wedding anniversary was very memorable. I wanted to make the event huge so I took Sheila hot-air ballooning. It was a fantastic experience. It was exciting because what you do in a hot-air balloon is trust the wind. In other words, there is not much you can do. You have to get the equipment right and a trained pilot is important but – in the end – it is all about how you catch the wind. As we floated over rural Kent we had to sort out many of the details as we went along: avoiding horses, cows and power lines were all important but ultimately we trusted our lives to the wind. To live 'real church' here you have to trust the Holy Spirit. Paul was doing life in the power of the Spirit in the middle of great community, living the emotions of fear and exasperation, openness to God and learning to live out of control. Yet he had the big stuff dead right. This was a life fixed to the earth, lived in the power of the Spirit and going into the world.

*The spectacular ordinary life flourishes in community.*

## Questions and Reflections

1. Where do you go when you feel 'totally inadequate' and/or 'scared to death'? Why do you do this?

2. What can you expect from your local church or Christian community? Are your expectations cynical? Are they naïve?

3. What do you think could be the real cost of avoiding some sort of community with other Christians?

# Mission

If you don't like change, you are going to like irrelevance
less.                                                    *Eric Shinseki*[17]

God has made two big moves so far: he has created and
redeemed. The universe was created from the love
between Father, Son and Spirit. Then Jesus came in the
flesh to die and rise again, bringing redemption to a
shattered world. This is God on the move, taking the initiative and doing his wonders in the world. This is God
in movement and mission.

Mission is not just an activity to be completed or a job
to be done. It is descriptive of all that God is, and therefore what we are called to be. For us this means the totality of our lives lived out in the world. This includes
words, deeds, thoughts, passions, prayers and responses lived out with other people. We engage in mission
because God's heart has taken hold of our hearts so,
through the church, mission is the overflow of God's
heart to the world. We are made for mission and when
we do not engage in acts of speech, mercy and justice
beyond ourselves we are reduced. We deflate like post-
Christmas balloons. We become undernourished and
eventually deformed if we do not reach out to the world

in acts of mercy, justice and evangelism. The truth is that the evil-shattering and life-enriching Jesus is to be worshipped through gossiping his name and deeds throughout the world. When we participate in this we grow in likeness to him.

The formation of a spectacular ordinary life takes place in movement towards the world. It is as we engage our gifts in response to a need that spiritual muscle is developed. Momentum and movement are critical in physical formation and it is the same in other areas of life. We grow as we engage. In reaching out we discover each other, God, and ourselves. In this process we learn much of what we need for the many tasks ahead and become bigger people.

## Mission with Jesus

The book of Mark was probably written for the urban and persecuted church in Rome. The early chapters present us with discipleship 'boot camp'; the apprenticeship and development of the disciples, moving them from being unaware of Jesus and his kingdom through to obedient and courageous barrier-breakers for the kingdom of God. The disciples had to learn what we all need to learn: what does a healthy person look like and how do you become one?

In Luke 2:34 there is a prophecy spoken over the baby Jesus by a devout man called Simeon. He said, 'This child is destined to cause the falling and rising of many in Israel'. In other words, the relationship that people have with this child will be decisive in their destruction on one hand, or their establishment on the other. It is saying that if you are going to be healthy then responding to him is critical. Pivotal in becoming healthy and remaining that way is your relationship with God through Jesus Christ.

Jesus is forming a community of healthy people who know how to live spectacular and ordinary. The first community Jesus formed was the disciples and, like all groups of people, they had their own unique shape and mix. We have four fishermen, one despised tax collector and a member of a radical and unpopular political party. They were all laymen (not a religious expert in sight), there were no teachers of Scripture, none of them were chosen for their communication gifts and none of them had much money or a business skill that could be classed as successful. But Jesus was in the process of forming them into a community that was going to change the world as they knew it. Before very long – but after the resurrection and the sending of the Holy Spirit – there is an accusation against these followers of Jesus. It was one of the best compliments they could ever have been paid. The high priest says, 'You have filled Jerusalem with your teaching' (Acts 5:28) and within thirty years of the death of Jesus the good news of Jesus had spread throughout the known world. Jesus called people to him and began the process of fashioning them into what he intended them to be. He called a disconnected, occasionally confused and weak group together and then transformed them into a people intent on changing the world. Mark 3:13–18 teaches us that three things take place.

## Designation: the Act of Speech

'He appointed twelve – designating them apostles.'

Can you imagine being male and called Vivian or Viv? Johnny Cash recorded a song called 'A Boy Named Sue'.

It is about a negligent father who calls his son Sue and then leaves him to deal with it. The son hates the name but it toughens him up to face the challenges of life. When he finally confronts his father in a bar Sue is told the reason why, 'I knew you'd have to get tough or die' says his father. But, being a Country and Western song, they still fight it out in the mud, the blood and the beer.

My name caused endless fights at school. Any dispute would eventually lead to 'At least I don't have a girl's name,' and then the fight would start all over again. A policeman asked me 'Where is your skirt?' after some minor cycling violation, and I was once booked into a ladies' ward for an operation on my nose. I had a moustache at the time.

I have had hockey tickets to see the Vancouver Canucks cancelled because the voice booking the seats over the phone was male, and the name on the credit card female. I have had telephone salesmen ask me if I resented my parents for giving me a name like that and others who just cackled down the line, safe in their anonymity. I have been asked after meetings where I have spoken, 'Is your name Vim, or Bim?' The local newspaper even refused to put my name under my own wedding picture, explaining that everyone would think they had made a mistake. The list goes on, but through it all I still love my name.

Your name shapes you. Whoever has the right to designate you is very powerful. The English language developed out of the mixed melting pot of conquerors and invaders that formed the English nation. This powerful and creative language is occasionally used destructively and the British tabloid press are the lords of this dark art. You need to have the hide of a rhino to stand in the middle of a tabloid onslaught when everything you are, say and do is examined or exposed in the popular press.

In England this attack appears to be one of the prices of celebrity. Who can forget the tabloid treatment of the English national football team manager, Graham Taylor? Taylor did fail to lead England through to the 1994 World Cup finals, but he did not do it by himself. However, one tabloid paper created a mocking cartoon of his head looking like a turnip and printed it on the back page. His international career never recovered. Every time I see him on the television, it is that image of his head as a turnip which comes to my mind. Graham Taylor was labelled in word and picture and his name became associated with the turnip. This name has stuck, shaping the popular image of what he did and who he is. Designating someone is a huge and important responsibility.

Jesus gathered his men together and named them. Their new name came to shape them, for much of what makes a person is in their name. The disciples were appointed and given the designation of Apostle and that is what they became. With that name came identity and responsibility. Jesus also did some other more specific naming at the same time. He renamed Simon and called him Peter. He renamed James and John, who were the sons of Zebedee, and gave them the name Boanerges, which means Sons of Thunder. It must change your life in some way if one day you know yourself as the son of Zebedee and then you get a new name celebrating a loud deep rumbling noise caused by rapid expansion of atmospheric gases which are suddenly heated by lightning!

One of the most startling changing of names in Scripture is that of Abram to Abraham. In the middle of massive changes in his life God says to Abram in Genesis 17:5 'No longer will you be called Abram [exalted Father]; your name will be Abraham, for I have made you a father of many nations'. Even Abraham's wife Sarai is renamed Sarah.

In *The Lion, the Witch and the Wardrobe* C.S. Lewis gives the children new names. These are names that call them out of themselves into another richer place. These renamings and new designations are blessings, not just to do with a person's job, but with their very nature.

Before Jesus sends us out into the world he gives us our designation. Deep down he names us so that we don't live out of technique or cleverness but from a deeper place to do with our true identity. Healthy Christian communities are always reflecting back to each other the name or names given to us by God.

Neil T. Anderson, in *The Steps to Freedom in Christ*, makes this list of some of the possible ways to understand who we are

I am the salt of the earth and the light of the world
(Mt. 5:13–14)

I am a branch of the true vine, Jesus, a channel of his life
(Jn. 15:1–5)

I have been chosen and appointed by God to bear fruit
(Jn. 15:16)

I am a personal, Spirit-empowered witness of Christ
(Acts 1:8)

I am a temple of God (1 Cor. 3:16)

I am a minister of reconciliation for God (2 Cor. 5:17–21)

I am God's fellow worker (2 Cor. 6:1)

I am seated with Christ in heavenly realms (Eph. 2:6)

I am God's workmanship, created for good works
(Eph. 2:10)

I may approach God with freedom and confidence
(Eph. 3:12)

I can do all things through Christ who strengthens me!
(Phil. 4:13)

To live a spectacular ordinary life and engage the world you need to grow into your understanding of your designation. This is not 'positive thinking'; it is the declaration of truth, the declaration of what God speaks over you and in your life.

How do you obtain your name or names through which you can live? Living in community is critical because naming is a communal act. It is as you work, worship and pray in community that you discover who you are. The community effectively names you. This is one of the reasons why developing healthy communities is such a crucial task. This communal response then interacts with your personal gifts and passions. What are the things you can and can't do? What moves you and what does not? In community you live out your desires, passions and burdens, discovering who you are in the middle of it. Listening to the voice of God is primary to hearing your designation and receiving his call on your life. If you do not pray or read Scripture you forget your name and lose track of what you are doing in the world.

## Hospitality: the Act of Embrace

'That they might be with him.'

Mission – like prayer – resembles breathing; without an inhalation there will be no exhalation. Crucial to the disciples' movement out into the world was their transformation in the presence of Jesus. When they said 'yes' to Jesus the disciples entered a world of welcome and invitation; they received his hospitality in receiving his embrace. Jesus performed his first miracle as an invited guest at a wedding and everything ends at the close of time at a wedding feast in a city of celebration. Celebration, hospitality and embrace are all vital virtues if we are going to engage the world and do it well.

Miroslav Volf, in his book *Exclusion and Embrace*,[18] brilliantly details the nature of a hug. In four Acts he traces what it means to reach out to anyone and try to show them love and welcome through an embrace

### Act one: Opening the Arms

Reaching for the other
Discontent with myself as I am
Expression of a void created by absence of this person
Expression of desire for the other person
I do not want to be alone
Expression of that which already exists within ourselves
Demonstration that I have created space for myself and the
    other person to enter
You step out of yourself into this space of embrace
It is a gesture of invitation

### Act two: Waiting

Self-initiated movement
Vulnerability
Halting at the boundaries
Waiting for desire in the other person to be ignited
The power of signalled desire is present
It is an indication that nothing is going to happen without reciprocity

### Act three: Closing the Arms

It takes two pairs of arms to make one embrace
In an embrace a host is a guest and a guest is a host

Each enters the space of the other
You feel the presence of the other
Your presence is felt
Appropriate touch that does not crush or become
      assimilated
Possess the power 'not-to-understand' through allowing
      the person the freedom to be another person

### Act four: Opening the Arms Again

The arms must open again so that the 'I' does not disappear
      into the undifferentiated 'we' of totalitarian control
Letting go offers the possibility of return. This can now
      happen again

Jesus called the disciples to be with him. He embraced them. This was an invitation of huge generosity to participate in his life. When you read the gospels you see a continual flow of interaction between the disciples and Jesus. He called them. They watch him. He asks them questions. He sends them out. They come back and report what happened. He challenges them. He addresses their fears. They live with the pressures of people's needs and persecution (Mk. 6). They were going to grow into a healthy community because they participated in the embrace and invitation of Jesus to be with him. In a similar way we will become healthy and fully-formed as we participate in each other's lives and enter into hospitality. If we are going to reach a world, and see it transformed, then this continual embrace of Jesus is pivotal. Without it, all of our attempts to change the world become dry and functional. With it we are able to remain full, supple and free in our engagement with the world. The difference is between night and day.

# Encounter: the Act of Departure

> 'That he might send them out to preach and that they might
> have authority to drive out demons.'

Every arrival is a point of departure. The disciples come
to Jesus so that they may go out. They are both
embraced and released on the spectacular ordinary journey ahead. They have to depart as Jesus sends them out
in mission and personal growth. In a similar way we are
formed as we are sent. Our lives are formed in the challenges, visions and burdens that God places in our path.
Departure is crucial in living a spectacular ordinary life;
you have to move on and into the world to live well. The
disciples' challenges are ours as well. They were called
to encounter people with the love and life of Jesus and
to encounter evil in all of its forms seeking to battle with
the world, the flesh and the Devil.

What were they to say when they went? They were to
say what Jesus said or something very similar. He said
'The kingdom of God is near. Repent and believe the
good news' (Mk. 1:15) and 'Come, follow me, and I will
make you fishers of men' (Mk. 1:17).

What were they to do? They were to encounter evil in
all of its guises. The authority given to them through
Jesus had to be exercised in response to evil in a way
similar to Jesus who 'travelled throughout Galilee,
preaching in their synagogues and driving out demons'
(Mk. 1:39). They engaged with personal and communal
evil. Jesus delivered people from demonic grip but also
challenged the demonic forces behind the systems of
evil. In challenging centres of evil Jesus kept the company of 'sinners' (Mk. 2:13–17), did not keep the normal
rules on fasting (Mk. 2:18–22) and healed someone on
the wrong day (Mk. 2:23 – 3:6). We should anticipate

similar challenging issues as we engage in mission. It will be challenging, messy and sometimes confusing, but it will also be significant or exhilarating, and often a combination of both.

So in the name of Jesus we speak truth over each other, open up our lives in acts of hospitality, embrace and say farewell. We say to each other that it is time for you to go. This is how Jesus did it. This is how he formed a healthy community of people who changed the world. Jesus releases us into the spectacular ordinary and the Spirit enables the ever-increasing transformation of life.

*The spectacular ordinary life moves out into the world taking faith risks.*

## Questions and Reflections

1. How do you feel about yourself? Do these feelings propel you towards a world in need or hold you back from it? What will you do if they hold you back?

2. Jesus re-designated the disciples and sent them out to do the works of God. What work do you want him to send you to do? What may get in the way of that?

3. What is your next intentional mission for God? Where will it take place? What will you do? Who will you do it with? Why are you doing it?

# The Life

So how do you live life? How do you live in such a way that the big life offered to the world through the death and resurrection of Jesus is not just frustrating because you can't do it, or becomes so focused on yourself that you are the main point of your own, often wonderful, sometimes tragic or occasionally tedious story? At the end of each chapter I have tried to sum up the main idea behind the thoughts and reflections. So we have

The spectacular ordinary life is encountering and flourishing in the love of the Father.

The spectacular ordinary life is discovering freedom through forgiveness.

The spectacular ordinary life is fully alive in the company of the Holy Spirit.

The spectacular ordinary life creatively engages the world.

The spectacular ordinary life healthily engages brokenness and the incomplete.

The spectacular ordinary life is fully present all the time, every day.

The spectacular ordinary life engages a world where everything can be redeemed.

The spectacular ordinary life is characterized by significance and celebration.

The spectacular ordinary life imagines the future and makes decisions rooted in hope.

The spectacular ordinary life flourishes in intimacy with God.

The spectacular ordinary life flourishes in community.

The spectacular ordinary life moves out into the world taking faith risks.

But to just gather up a series of principles and seek to apply them to your life will not deliver the spectacular ordinary life as God intended. Mere principles and good ideas can be hard rocks on which to crash. From a distance they look so attractive, but in the end they cause shipwrecks. Good principles, intentions and ideas can leave you feeling disappointment or experiencing intense guilt, because the idea was great but far away from the reality of your own life. Being forced to live up to ideals through social expectation, fear or insecurity is the devil's work and has caused endless trouble in people's lives.

So, at the core of the spectacular ordinary life are not principles or great ideas, but a fully-lived relationship with Father, Son and Spirit. Jesus prayed, 'Father, just as

you are in me and I am in you. May they also be in us
. . . I in them and you in me . . .' (Jn. 17:21–3) and in doing
so explained the nature of a wonderful life. Life is participation in the relationship with Father, Son and Spirit.
This relationship is our true home. This is where we are
fully accepted, loved and released to be all that we could
possibly be. It is in this relationship that we become like
Jesus, who has shown us how to live life to the full. The
more Jesus-shaped we are the more alive we are. It is
amazing that we don't fall to the ground jelly-legged or
spontaneously combust with the wonder and richness of
it all. So what does the spectacular ordinary life look
like?


## Story-rich

Poverty can be expressed in many ways, as can wealth,
but a person who is living a spectacular ordinary life is
always heading towards the world of the story-rich. This
does not mean that they are great at telling stories or that
they have an imagination that can make them up. It is
that they know their own story and live it in the middle
of the big story of God, both weaving into each other.
The story of God's grace and love is textured into their
celebrations as well as into their day-to-day experience.
There is no gap between natural and supernatural,
material and spiritual. There is just life lived with God,
in the middle of our stories, with the mundane and the
miraculous all part of God's purpose for our lives.
Through each succeeding decade this story becomes
richer, fuller and broader like an ever-widening, full and
mighty river.

## God-focused

People who live a spectacular ordinary life live humbly and lovingly in relation to Father, Son and Spirit. This means they understand in their heads, and increasingly know in their hearts, that the centre of life is God and not themselves. This inevitably leads to worship. Worship means that there is another centre other than myself. I am drawn out of myself and into love and encounter with God. This enables my heart to grow, my head to be full of imagination and my whole being to be caught up in continual thankfulness. This leads to rich conversation with God. God speaks and we respond. God's voice comes to us primarily and authoritatively through Scripture, but also through vision, dream, words given to the church at a particular moment, angelic visitation and all the other ways in which Scripture explains that God speaks.

## Flourishing Identity

When we encounter this sort of life a clear sense of identity begins to emerge. This identity is not primarily to do with money, house, breeding or nationality. It is identity rooted in community. We come to live and know that we are made for one another. We are released from the contemporary isolating trap where we only find our identity in ourselves, our particular gifting and specific achievements. This is really difficult for many of us but it is really important if we want to live a spectacular ordinary life. We learn that everything about us is plural if we want to live well. We live with each other and with Father, Son and Spirit. Therefore we do not live life alone. We discover that all of what we are and what we are to become is unfolded to us as we walk with God and community.

## Engaged Restoration

Joyful, realistic and fully-embraced repentance characterizes the spectacular ordinary life. This is not merely the repentance relating to specific sins that have emerged through satanic plots or our own nature; sins that come along with the various addictions and temptations that seek to rule our lives. It is living openly, honestly and vulnerably with God, all of the time. Life comes to people when they know the way back to God through the cross and resurrection of Jesus Christ. They know what to do when they have messed things up through sin and stupidity. But the gospel offers more than this. We are fully alive and live in the spectacular ordinary when each moment is lived in brokenness and joyful humility before God. This does not mean that we always have to be thinking particularly religious thoughts. It does mean that, in the wonder of a relationship sustained by Father, Son and Spirit, we live and rest in humble brokenness. Rather than this crushing or defeating us, the opposite takes place. It is in the place of this sort of repentance and humility that we are released into faith-filled, confident yet broken living.

## Creative Exploration

The spectacular ordinary life is lived in creativity. This is not just for the elite who have the time to produce art, play music or go to the theatre. It is to do with the way we have been made. Each of us has been given the image of God and, because God creates, so we can create as well. Our job is to play. The spectacular ordinary life joyfully plays and experiments with all the creativity given to us. We take the gifts he has given us and just see how far they can go as we fully live them through faith, imagination and in connecting our lives to the community. There are no limits to the possibilities when this happens. Any limits will be self-imposed. We do not know how God is going to work out our lives and what will be their true effect, but when we join our hearts, heads and hands with others the sky provides no limit. The six billion people who inhabit our planet need the church to grasp this so that the news of freedom in Christ may be theirs as well as ours.

## Inner Journey

To live a spectacular ordinary life there has to be an inner journey. This is the unfolding discovery of who I am and what I am becoming, as I journey with God and other people in the world each day. To live life well there is always an ongoing reflection regarding your internal world. At times this can be a big stretch, and it is always a long journey. We can only do this well with the help of the Holy Spirit who switches the lights on in our heads and hearts, letting us know what is straight and what is bent, and therefore what needs fixing sooner or later. We cannot fully undertake this journey without seriously encountering Christian Scripture in a contemplative form and without some form of community. Merely having Bible information in our heads does not always help. Scripture has to become food to us, sustaining our inner lives just as bread sustains the body.

## Body Keeping

Not all of us have healthy bodies. Our bodies are a gift to us and full health is a privilege. Yet a spectacular ordinary life is lived well when we look after the remarkable material that is our body and the environment in which we move. Eating, sleeping, working, exercising and relaxing are some of the things we do with our bodies and all of them are critical in how we encounter life. This is the case regardless of what kind of body we have. Neglect or difficulty in these areas always causes some problem or another. We can become vulnerable to temptations, sins and dark forces if we choose to abuse our own bodies. If we treat our bodies well then our lives are set up for the particular challenges of each day, be they spectacular, ordinary or a combination of both.

## Integrated Purpose

A spectacular ordinary life integrates process and success. Knowing that we cannot be more of a success than God has already made us brings great freedom. We can achieve our goals and enjoy all the money and power that stream from our success. But in the end we know the main focus is the process of becoming all God intends us to be. This cannot be reduced to money, houses, cars, yachts and two skiing holidays a year. We grow to understand that what we regard as a great success, God sees as part of the process of getting to where he wants us to be. If we catch a vision of our lives in these terms we can fully celebrate our successes but not become victims to the intoxicating, binding and poisonous sin of pride.

## Emotional Resilience

In the ever-changing, challenging and intense world in which many of us live, stress characterizes our response. In this world, emotional resilience is critical, because the people who are able to cope with uncertainty will, in the end, flourish. Entering into the spectacular ordinary life delivers this sort of emotional resilience, and allows room for elasticity under the pressures of change, suffering and conflict. Living the big story in relationship with God and others gives us the framework for our lives. This resilience comes from fully living the whole of the story given to us in Scripture. If we reduce the story – through not taking parts of Scripture seriously – then we will damage our capacity to live well. It is only when we live with Father, Son, Spirit, creation, fall, incarnation, redemption, ascension and future hope in a context of communion, community and mission that the framework is big enough to enable us to understand the nature of our own stresses and pressures, and live resilient toughened-up lives.

## Deepening Friendship

In the end everything leads back to Father, Son and Spirit who are in a relationship of the deepest possible love and friendship. Here is a mighty and transforming vision, for it lets us know where the centre of everything lies. Jesus came to re-establish friendship with us and God. The spectacular ordinary life embraces that fully. Through the cross and resurrection Satan is defeated and we have become friends of God. This friendship is characterized by grace and love being poured over our lives like sweet-smelling oil. Through the cross and resurrection we are able to know that the intention of God is to re-make us into his likeness through encountering his loving friendship and overwhelming grace. This is the gravitational pull of everything and brings us to the point of submission and prayer.

*This is the spectacular ordinary life.*

# Cultivating a Spectacular
# Ordinary Life

Life of any kind is a gift of God. So you can't just conjure life up in some act of self-assertion, you have to be gifted life by God. However, there are things you can do and practices to engage in that put you in the way of God so you can receive life. These are the practices, disciplines and rhythms of the church that we know can bring the life of God if he wants to give it to us. Generation after generation around the world have found spectacular ordinary life in these practices, so they are critical for us if we are to live well.

I now live just two hundred paces from the Thames and I walk by it whenever I can. Two hundred paces in the opposite direction and I can walk down the Fulham Palace Road. The two are very different. Fulham Palace Road is almost always clogged, like a drain after a summer storm, with traffic edging along towards Hammersmith Broadway. It is normal for the traffic to go slower than walking pace and often stop altogether while fumes pump and frustration mounts. In the other direction is the stunning river with its seven metres of tidal rise and fall, abundant wildlife, people enjoying themselves, magnificent sunsets and huge sense of space.

Every day I can choose to walk down either the road or the river, and whenever I can, I choose the river. The river walk always inspires, opens and excites, while the road tends to have the opposite effect. If you want a spectacular ordinary life similar choices have to be made and practices engaged. To put it starkly, do you want to go along the river that transforms your life and imagination, or just engage with the frustration and fumes?

What are the practices, disciplines and rhythms that bring about a spectacular ordinary life? There is a huge heritage at this point. Many have gone this way before. Of the contemporary writers you can read Richard Foster's *Celebration of Discipline*, Dallas Willard's *The Spirit of the Disciplines* and Tony Jones' *The Sacred Way* for some brilliant insights, well-presented and occasionally controversial ideas. I don't wish to repeat their work. Rather, I want to explain what has been effective for me as a white, widely-travelled Englishman born in the fifties whose experience of life has been mostly joyful and always urban. I don't share these thoughts so that you can admire how well I do this, for, as Eugene Peterson keeps telling us, there are no experts in the spiritual life. I share them in the sense that this is the shape I am in, and for better or worse this is how I think it happened. Everyone's journey is different along the path to transformation.

## Practice One: Scripture Meditation

Engaging in regular meditation on Scripture is a very ordinary act but is spectacular in effect. This is where you take a passage of Scripture and read it slowly, while being open to the voice of the Holy Spirit to enlarge your heart and open it up. This brings about what could be called a 'thin place'; the place where there is little distance between you and God. This is the place of God-encounter or the place where we find God's heart in his word, and where we meet God on God's terms. Bernard of Clairvaux said

> Store up the Word of God as you would food. The Word of God is a living bread, the food of the soul. Bread kept in a cupboard can be stolen, eaten by rats, go stale but once it is eaten none of these misfortunes are to be feared. Store up the Word of God like that, because blessed are those that keep it. Let it sink into your inmost heart and pass into your affections and way of life. Eat plentifully of it and your soul will rejoice. Never forget to eat this bread, lest your heart wither, but feed and strengthen it with so rich and fruitful a food. If you hold on to the Word the Word will protect you. The Son of God will come to you and his Father also.

I first moved into Scripture meditation when I was twenty-one. A visiting lecturer at a college I was attending taught me how to do it and nothing has been the same since. Bible study is critical. You need to know what Scripture says and means without imposing your own ideas on the text. But Bible study is not enough. If you are to grow you need to read Scripture so that it will *form* you and not just *inform* you. This is the place of 'holy leisure' where you allow a passage to wash over you and through you, while opening up to the voice of the Holy Spirit. This is where Scripture becomes food to you, shaping your head, heart and will.

This is also a place of prayer. If I only pray about what is on my heart, or on my agenda, my prayer is inevitably very limited. I do need to bring to God all that is going on in my life; all my concerns, but I also want to be taken into a much bigger place and this happens through meditative, prayerful reading of Scripture.

For instance, recently my wife read the story of the landowner who went out in the morning to hire workers for his farm (Mt. 20) so I quote – with permission – from her prayer journal. Note the transformational nature of her interactions with Scripture and the Holy Spirit.

I've known this story all my life, having grown up in a Christian home. But this time I read it contemplatively, using my *imagination* and noticing my *feelings*. This is very important for my feelings tell me what is going on inside me. As I spent time with this story, I began to notice how *unfair* it was that the landowner started to pay the men hired at the end of the day, the same wage as those he hired early in the morning and he did it right in front of those who were hired early. I noticed I *felt* irritated by this. This was all brought into my prayer. I stayed with this story and realized this is about the Kingdom of God and God isn't fair, he's generous. I was able to see I am not as generous as my heavenly father and this was brought into prayer. Throughout the following weeks, I continued to contemplate this story and I noticed how I had identified with the man hired early in the day. I have been a Christian since I was a child and I realized I have a tendency to self-righteousness. Through this type of prayerful reading the Lord was revealing my heart to me in a way I would not have noticed if I had just read this story again quickly and moved on. I realized there were echoes of the older brother in the story of the prodigal son. I, as a Christian of long-standing, was inclined to think I deserve more than those who have not followed the Lord as long as I have. This was a wonderful insight into my own heart, for which I felt so grateful. This did not condemn me, it enabled me to have a much more honest talk with the Lord about my own heart and I was reminded how generous my heavenly father is. This is the type of experience we can have as we read Scripture prayerfully, contemplatively, noticing our feelings and using our imaginations. Our conversation with the Lord can become so much more honest and deep. And as I notice areas of my life which still need to be transformed, it makes me much less judgmental of others who are still struggling in areas of their lives.

There is no special technique here. Anyone can do it, but it is not always easy. In the middle of it you sometimes have either no thoughts you consider are worth thinking through, or a torrent of responses to the voice of the Spirit through the text. Sometimes, in the middle of this, I get mundane ideas regarding how my day should go, who I should phone, what I should avoid and who I should seek to really bless. Often there is insight regarding what I need to pray about in the national and international arenas. Frequently there is some insight about my own life. Some of these are the Holy Spirit bringing back something familiar and at other times something completely new. Generally this is a place of intense creativity for me. The central question here is: do you want to listen to God and are you ready to be alone to do it? Jesus went to a lonely place so he could talk with his Father and so must we (Mt. 14:13).

## Practice Two: Prayer

If Scripture meditation is about inhalation then prayer is about exhalation. Prayer is about breathing out the desires of a life touched by God. Yet Scripture meditation and prayer are so closely intertwined it is difficult to neatly divide between the two. But as I encounter God through prayer two things change; the world in which I live and the way I live in the world. Prayer not only changes things but prayer changes me. Prayer brings us into Jesus-shape.

I had much of my formation around prayer developed through my twenty-eight years with Operation Mobilisation. Full nights of prayer, half nights of prayer, prayer weeks, prayer days and prayer times were part of the intercessory diet of OM All this was done under the assumption that we were 'God's fellow workers' (1 Cor 3:9) which meant that God was including us in the way in which he shaped the world. Much of it was to do with spiritual warfare and living a healthy vigorous life of spiritual revolution. As a community we were going to engage God, Scripture, prayer and then the world through mission.

So for me, prayer is not just engagement with an order of service given to you – even though that can sometimes be helpful – it is the bringing of God's burdens back to him in rich heartfelt conversation. It is to do with allowing the Holy Spirit to bring to you the thoughts of God and you pray them. You can do this in any location and at any time.

## Practice Three: Learning

Learning has played a huge part in the development of my own life. Romans 12:2 teaches us that we should not be conformed to the world but transformed by the renewing of our minds. John 8:32 tells us that truth sets us free. If you want a renewed mind and freedom, learning is a significant part of the process.

What we learn and how we learn it is pivotal in the way in which we are all formed. We are all in the process of being schooled by something even if we don't know it. Advertising agencies seek out ways to address and flatter us so that we purchase their product. We are all being shaped in one way or another by the Nike swoosh and L'Oreal's message that we are 'worth it'. We are all learning in one way or another and being formed by it as we go. I know I am. So we have to take our learning seriously if we want to develop a spectacular ordinary life. What do we want to put into our heads and allow to form our imaginations? I was listening to a Chinese doctor on the radio and in one phrase he brought together much of the controversy around obesity, over-eating and nutrition. His phrase, 'in China we understand food as medicine' has helped me see eating as self-medication: a way I had never seen it before. He was saying that if you want a healthy body you need to eat the right foods. It is exactly the same for your mind.

Reading, listening, watching, conversation, asking questions and challenging accepted values have been part of my growth. But this does not mean it is easy. Learning is sometimes painful, often frustrating and adds responsibility to your life. But as Richard Foster says, 'Many Christians remain in bondage to fears and anxieties simply because they do not avail themselves of the Disciplines of study.'[19] Along with the vast majority of us, I have been blessed with the ability to study and find out what is going on in the world. There is no life in choosing ignorance.

Learning includes the totality of life. You don't have to have had a formal education to be able to learn. Just being with people, reflecting on their lives and having the courage to ask questions opens up a rich world.

Being able to trace what God has done in creation opens up a whole world of truth and revelation. I would never have thought that, while standing on Spanish

Banks overlooking Vancouver, a big question in my head would be resolved through observing two birds. But as I reflected on the variety of creation I could see afresh that there was room for two distinct ways of approaching a particular problem and both of them were valid. If you want to grow a spectacular ordinary life, ask for a deep hunger for learning.

## Practice Four: Humility

This is difficult, but vital if you are a person similar to me because humility demands vulnerability. Thirty years ago another word that explains my use of the word vulnerability would be 'brokenness'. Roy Hession's book *The Calvary Road* marked out the path for this 'brokenness'. It is to do with living an open confessional life that seeks to be as truthful as possible both to people and to God. When this sort of brokenness and vulnerability is pursued as a discipline it is really an attack on personal sin and particularly the sin of pride.

Everything within us – within me – wants to avoid vulnerability and brokenness. If you tell people the truth about your thoughts or some of your deeds it looks like weakness, loss of face and makes people think badly of you. At first glance it seems much better to pursue self-promotion and give everyone an image of strength and victory. But often the opposite is the case. You tell someone about your pride, love of money, sexual temptations and suchlike, and the effect is often very different to the one you anticipated. Vulnerability and confession often bring about strength more than weakness, and encouragement more than shame. This means choosing a life of repentance in which you joyfully accept the mercy of God into your heart and over your life every day. It also means resisting and denying dark forces that want to drag you through the filth of your own arrogant imagination and self-focus through to the freedom that wonderful repentance brings.

Beware at this point. Humility is not an excuse for being passive or stepping back from the call of God on your life. True humility embraces what God says about you and is focused on not living any less or any more than that. God's work is done in the middle of confession, brokenness, vulnerability, weakness and the incomplete. Practising humility calls for a life of confession of sin but also a life of exhilarating steps of faith.

## Practice Five: Rest

Probably the first move in developing a spectacular ordinary life is rest. Rest and faith are closely linked together. Being able to rest means that I can trust God is doing what I cannot do and working where I cannot work. Rest can be very hard work at least in the initial stages. As you take your learning and prayer seriously, so you also need to take your rest seriously. For me this means solitude, observing Sabbath, spending time with my wife, occasional movies and keeping fit.

I am energized by people. Writing a book is a discipline for me because I have to spend so much time alone with my laptop, desk and chair. But to really rest I need to avoid loneliness and enter into solitude. What is the difference? Loneliness is when I am on my own in isolation. Solitude is when I am away from people and keeping the company of Father, Son and Spirit. The twin of solitude is silence, where you choose to say nothing. This is truly a discipline for me but an important one. This solitude and silence, when lived in communion with Father, Son and Spirit, is both restful and creative at the same time. Urban life demands times of solitude and silence so we can rest well.

Sabbath is another part of rest. I am still working on this even though there is so much focus on this in Scripture. The practice is to take a day and give it to God. You step out of a world of initiative, personal drive and being in control, stepping instead into a world where God is in control and saying and doing whatever is on his mind. If during these times God says nothing that's fine, but the focus is on hanging around and allowing the Holy Spirit to make the conversation. But, when connected up with the other disciplines, there is usually much conversation going on.

I rest well when I feel I am at home. I often feel 'at home' with many people around the world because home is not just place but a series of relationships where there is acceptance and love. But I am 'at home' the most when I am with my wife. This is a huge privilege for me and one that many people long for. With her I rest.

Developing a spectacular ordinary life means being intentional about rest. You rest in such a way that you don't merely indulge and become slothful but discover energy and renewal that propels you forward to live the call of God on your life.

## Practice Six: Community

You cannot develop a spectacular ordinary life alone, even though silence and solitude do help. We are made for community and find our life in relationship with others. What does this mean in practice? For me it means having a friend who accompanies me on my walk with God, being part of a small group, living local church as fully as possible and spending time with friends who I have loved over many years.

One of the joys of my life is being a spiritual director to some people. Being a spiritual director or spiritual friend means accompanying people as they walk with God. In these particular relationships the focus is on seeking to recognize what God is doing in the other person's life. There is rarely any actual direction given but often you help people notice the road they are on and alternative roads they could choose. It is different from counselling and mentoring, the latter of which I do regularly. I also have the joy of having a spiritual director who does the same for me. Each of us needs someone who will walk with us in our walk with God. This person will generally be wise, loving and indifferent to your life but a crucial part of your communal life.

Membership of some sort of small group is critical and I have been part of many. They are normally church-based and give you the opportunity to give your life to others who you would not usually be drawn to at a social event. I am also the member of a small group that is not a Bible study or prayer meeting, but the meeting of a group of friends, in this case four married couples. In this group the agenda is tracing how God has shaped us since we last met. We spend much time listening to each others' stories and asking questions. It has been for all of us a rich, powerful encounter with each other and God. So much life and goodness has been released through this small gathering.

Being a member of a local church has been pivotal in my life of community. I have been a member or leader of seven local churches over the last forty years. All of them have been great communities and all of them have been flawed in one way or another. One I had to leave because it was so wounding to be there, I could not take it anymore. But the church community is critical in developing the spectacular ordinary life. Living local church well demands discipline and commitment. The mix of people offers diversity, love, challenge and gives you a base from which to move out into your world. This is also the place where you can practise the discipline of submission where you listen to others, engage with teaching and don't insist on your own agenda being the agenda for everyone else.

## Practice Seven: Journey

Considerable travel has been part of my life since I was in my mid-twenties. I have been to so many places. Someone once asked me when I was going to settle down, without realizing that this style of life was settled as far as I was concerned. I met my wife on the biggest journey I have ever undertaken. Forty-five of us travelled on a six-week journey overland from Brussels to Asia via Europe, Turkey, Iran, Afghanistan, Pakistan and eventually India. It was a vivid experience, an extravaganza of different foods, cultures, attitudes and weather. I have not stopped travelling since. The discipline of going has always shaped my life.

Journey is crucial in developing a spectacular ordinary life. Each day is a journey offering up huge possibilities; each life is a journey with its twists and turns along the road. But to engage the journey well you need to practise journey and learn to do it well. Yet, you can stay in one geographic place the whole of your life and do this sort of journeying well. The truth is that even if we don't like journeying the aging process drives us along, shifting how we perceive the world and how people perceive us, so journey we must, like it or not.

The journey to hospitality has been a wonderful one. Over the last twenty-five years we have had the sort of house that enabled us to have people stay. We have had many wonderful lodgers and hundreds of guests. Through opening up our home we have had such a good time! It has also opened up the possibility of acts of service for me. I was thirteen when I felt God say he wanted me to preach and teach and that is what has happened. The journey has been about pursuing God's call on my heart and it has been a rich journey. As with the hospitality, I have had such a good time!

The big journey is the one out into the world: the refocusing of your life outside of self and heading off to a broken world. No one life is big enough to satisfy itself. We all need to stretch out and reach damaged and dislocated people through mighty speech and deeds as shown in the book of Acts. If you are going to grow a spectacular ordinary life you need to journey out of yourself and into the world.

## Practice Nine: Celebration

Celebration is a discipline I really want! This is a practice that is core to all the other practices, for a fundamental call on each Christian is living a thankful life. Joy is a fruit of the Spirit (Gal. 5:22) and gives us strength (Neh. 8:10) and is intended to lead us into a life of celebration and adoration of God.

Celebration is a choice. Such is the grip of cynicism on Western cultures that we often forget this. Since childhood I have been brought up to question, doubt, analyse and research every motive of anyone who looks or wants to do good. This cynicism is like clinging seaweed, pulling us down to drown when we should be swimming freely and joyfully. So we must learn to celebrate and become well-practised in it. If you want to live well you must disavow cynicism as you would stealing or murder.

A core practice here is being part of a community that celebrates the death and resurrection of Jesus through the act of Holy Communion or the Lord's Supper. It is from this meal that all other celebrations, dinner parties, birthday parties and anniversaries should take their cue. The reason why we are able to celebrate all the other events – and party so well – is because of the great celebration of the death and resurrection of Jesus, which has defeated Satan, proclaimed the end to fear and released us from our sins. If you want to live a spectacular ordinary life you need to be present at acts of the celebration of the death and resurrection of Jesus on a regular basis.

There are two other areas around celebration that I want to explain, as they are both important in my own life; praise and generosity. A celebratory life leads to the deliberate adoration of God where you give him praise. This can be worked out in many ways, but personally I just love Sundays at my own church when God-focused and skilled musicians lead the congregation in praise. This can sometimes be very loud or almost silent but praise it is. These times of obedient praise can be transformational because you meet with God as you engage head, heart and body in thanking him for all he has done in Jesus Christ. Linked with the practice of celebration is the practice of generosity. When you celebrate, your heart is transformed and you are opened up. Love is released, and giving becomes the most delightful and obvious thing in the world.

For all of its many weaknesses these are the practices that help move me along the road to full life. Others may tell a different story, but this is mine. It is just remarkable how in millions of lives God can take something very ordinary, and make it truly spectacular.

# Bibliography

Anderson, Neil T., *The Steps to Freedom in Christ* (Ventura: Regal Books, 2004).

Anthony, Metropolitan, *School for Prayer* (London: Darton, Longman and Todd, 1989).

Campolo, Tony, *The Kingdom of God is a Party* (Nashville: Thomas Nelson, 1992).

Doctrine Commission of the General Synod of the Church of England, *Being Human: A Christian Understanding of Personhood Illustrated with Reference to Power, Money, Sex and Time* (London: Church Publishing House, 2003).

Erickson, Millard J., *Christian Theology* (Grand Rapids: Baker, 1998²).

Foster, Richard J., *Celebration of Discipline: The Path to Spiritual Growth* (New York: HarperCollins, 2002).

Foster, Richard J., *The Challenge of the Disciplined Life: Christian Reflections on Money, Sex and Power* (New York: HarperCollins, 1989).

Grenz, Stanley J., *Theology for the Community of God* (Grand Rapids: Wm B. Eerdmans Publishing Co., 2000).

Hendriksen, William John: *New Testament Commentary* (Grand Rapids: Baker, 1953).

Hession, Roy, *The Calvary Road* (Fort Washington: CLC, 1964).

Jones, Tony, *The Sacred Way: Spiritual Practices for Everyday Life* (Grand Rapids: Zondervan, 2005).

Lloyd, Michael, *Café Theology: Exploring Love, the Universe and Everything* (London: Alpha International, 2005).

Nouwen, Henri J. M., *The Return of the Prodigal Son: A Story of Homecoming* (New York: Doubleday, 1994).

Peck, John and Charles Strohmer, *Uncommon Sense: God's Wisdom for our Complex and Changing World* (The Wise Press, 2001).

Peters, Tom, *Re-imagine!* (London: Dorling Kindersley, 2003).

Peterson, Eugene H., *Answering God: The Psalms as Tools for Prayer* (New York: HarperCollins, 1991).

Peterson, Eugene H., *Christ Plays in Ten Thousand Places: A Conversation in Spiritual Theology* (Grand Rapids: Wm. B. Eerdmans Publishing Co., 2006).

Pohl, Christine D., *Making Room: Recovering Hospitality as a Christian Tradition* (Grand Rapids: Wm. B. Eerdmans Publishing Co., 1999).

Smail, Tom, *Like Father Like Son* (Milton Keynes: Paternoster, 2005).

Vanier, Jean, *An Ark for the Poor* (New York: Crossroad, 1995).

Volf, Miroslav, *Exclusion and Embrace: A Theological Exploration of Identity, Otherness and Reconciliation* (Nashville: Abingdon Press, 1994).

Volf, Miroslav, *Free of Charge: Giving and Forgiving in a Culture Stripped of Grace* (Grand Rapids: Zondervan, 2006).

Walker, Andrew, and Luke Bretherton (eds), *Remembering Our Future: Explorations in Deep Church* (Milton Keynes: Paternoster, 2007).

Willard, Dallas, *Hearing God: Developing a Conversational Relationship with God* (Downers Grove: InterVarsity Press, 1999).

Willard, Dallas, *The Spirit of the Disciplines: Understanding How God Changes Lives* (New York: HarperCollins, 1988).

# Endnotes

1. The panda joke, made famous by Lynne Truss in her 2003 book, *Eats, Shoots & Leaves* (London: Profile Books).
2. This affirmation of love from Father to Son is a fulfilment of Isaiah 42:1—4.
3. In *Free of Charge: Giving and Forgiving in a Culture Stripped of Grace* (Grand Rapids: Zondervan, 2005, p. 70), Miroslav Volf states, 'Some theologians think of the three divine persons in the way that some ancients thought about the Three Graces of Greco-Roman antiquity – one for bestowing a benefit, one for receiving it, and a third for returning it. According to this pattern, the Father would give, the Son would receive, and the Holy Spirit would return. It is more likely, however, that each divine person gives, each receives, and each returns. Each loves and glorifies the other two, and each receives love and glory from them. One does not give first, with the result that the others would be indebted, but all give in the eternally moving circle of exchange. And because they give this way, they have all things in common except that which distinguishes them from each other. Their eternal bliss is the delight of this loving gift of exchange.'
4. Peter's examination in John 21:15–17 demonstrates the importance of responding well to the love of God. The response is to love him and the people created by him.

5 Hendricksen, William, *John: New Testament Commentary* (Grand Rapids: Baker, 1953, p. 159–160).

6 Lloyd, Michael, *Café Theology: Exploring Love, the Universe and Everything* (London: Alpha International, 2005), p. 61.

7 The Church defined the incarnation at the Council of Chalcedon in 451AD by declaring that Christ is true God and true man consubstantial with the Father in all things as to His divinity, yet in His humanity like unto us in all things, sin excepted.

8 Erickson, Millard, J., *Christian Theology* (Grand Rapids: Baker, 1998²).

9 Lloyd, *Café Theology*, p. 230.

10 Campolo, Tony, *The Kingdom of God is a Party* (Nashville: Thomas Nelson, 1992).

11 It was Henri Nouwen who articulated the trio of 'Communion, Community and Mission.' I was gripped as I watched a poor-quality DVD of Nouwen speaking at a conference in America. A similar scheme is explained by Karl Barth, who under the overall heading of 'Glorify' explained the importance of 'Gather, Grow and Go.' It is this later scheme that informs and shapes the life of St. Paul's in Hammersmith.

12 Anthony, Metropolitan, *School for Prayer* (London: Darton, Longman and Todd, 1989, p. 104).

13 Peterson, Eugene H., *Answering God* (New York: Harper Collins, 1991, p. 27).

14 Peterson, Eugene H., *Christ Plays in Ten Thousand Places*: A Conversation in Spiritual Theology (Grand Rapids: Wm. B. Eerdmans Publishing Co., p. 79).

15 Pohl, Christine D., *Making Room: Recovering Hospitality as a Christian Tradition* (Grand Rapids: Wm. B. Eerdmans Publishing Co., 1999, p. 34.

16 Philippians 4:14–20 and 2 Corinthians 11:8–9.

17 In Peters, Tom, *Re-imagine!* (London: Dorling Kindersley, 2003, p. 17).

[18] Volf, Miroslav, *Exclusion and Embrace: A Theological Exploration of Identity, Otherness and Reconciliation* (Nashville: Abindgon Press, 1996).

[19] Forster, Richard J., *Celebration of Discipline: The Path to Spiritual Growth* (New York: HaperCollins, 2002, p. 78.